I HEARD IT LIKE THIS

The Wisdom of Masahisa Goi

I HEARD IT LIKE THIS

The Wisdom of Masahisa Goi

Compiled by
HIDEO TAKAHASHI

BYAKKO PRESS

ISBN10: 4-89214-164-X
ISBN 13: 978-4-89214-164-5

Published by Byakko Press
812-1 Hitoana, Fujinomiya-shi,
Shizuoka-ken, 418-0102, Japan
tel: (+81) 544-29-5100; fax: (+81) 544-29-5116
http://www.byakkopress.ne.jp
e-mail: e-editor@byakkopress.ne.jp

Originally published as *Nyozegamon* (Byakko Press, 1966)

Translated from the Japanese by:
Koji Aiba, Kinuko Hamaya, Seiji Hashimoto,
Masato Hiramoto, Mako Ishibashi, Larissa Kasian,
Mary McQuaid, Tadao Miyoshi, Eiko Narazaki,
Grace Roberts, Kaoru Sasaki, and Caroline Uchima.

Cover photo and design by Mariana Chiarella
e-mail: foto@marianachiarella.com

About the Authors

Masahisa Goi

Born in Tokyo, Japan on November 22, 1916, Masahisa Goi was a poet, philosopher, writer, and singer. Though he aimed at a career in music, he found himself spontaneously drawn to the realms of philosophy and spiritual guidance. At the age of thirty he attained oneness with his divine self.

Mr. Goi authored more than 60 books and volumes of poetry, including *God and Man* (his first and most fundamental work), *The Spirit of Lao Tsu*, *Essays on the Bible*, *How to Develop Your Spirituality*, *The Way to the White Light*, *One Who Unites Heaven and Earth* (his autobiography), and *The Future of Mankind*—to name a few. Of these, *God and Man*, *One Who Unites Heaven and Earth*, *The Spirit of Lao Tsu*, and *The Future of Mankind* have been published in English. Translations of other works are now in progress.

Before departing from this world in 1980, he named Mrs. Masami Saionji, his adopted daughter, as his successor and leader of the world peace prayer movement that he initiated.

Hideo Takahashi

Hideo Takahashi was born in Tokyo and currently lives in Ichikawa City, Japan. For more than thirty years, he served as chief editor and assistant to the Japanese philosopher and peace visionary, Masahisa Goi. He has also authored more than twelve books of his own, including several volumes of original poetry and the well-known *Takemusu-Aiki*, which he co-authored with Morihei Ueshiba, the founder of Aikido.

Through his lectures and writings, Mr. Takahashi has worked extensively in Japan and other countries to promote a worldwide awareness of peace. In his spare time, he enjoys gardening, Aikido, and Japanese calligraphy.

Preface

I have heard that the Buddhist sutras open with the word *Nyozegamon*, which means 'I heard it like this.' Since this book, like the sutras, is filled with inspired words from a great spiritual teacher, it seemed to me that 'I Heard It Like This' might be a suitable title for it.

The phrases in this book were spoken by Masahisa Goi (whom we usually call 'Goi Sensei') in casual moments, as we walked together near our office, or stood on a platform waiting for a train, or chatted during breaks in the Byakko* publication room. Since his words always impressed me deeply, I made a habit of writing them down just as I heard them.

At first, I simply entered his sayings in my diary for personal use. Later, however, I came to feel that that they might benefit many others, and so I started to publish a few of them each month in *Byakko* magazine.

Even now, whenever I reread them, my heart is illuminated by the marvelous wisdom of Goi Sensei's words, which are truly light itself. Perhaps this I why I decided not to try to edit them, or produce a highly polished volume. Instead, I wanted to offer his words to you just as I heard them, believing that whichever page you turn to in the book, you will find gems worth treasuring.

When you feel sad, lonely, troubled, overwhelmed, or depressed, just think of Goi Sensei and open this book. Wherever your fingers may fall, I believe that you will find the words that are right for you at that time—words that will straighten your heart and fill you with brightness, courage, and a sublime sense of oneness or bliss.

Believing that they indeed hold this kind of mysterious power and wisdom, I offer you the words of Goi Sensei, just as I heard them.

Hideo Takahashi,
December 22, 1966

* *Byakko* literally means 'white light.' Masahisa Goi founded an organization called Byakko Shinko Kai, which introduces his teachings and offers spiritual practices to interested people.

The Wisdom of Masahisa Goi

✤ 1 ✤

The shortest path to happiness is to leave everything up to the love of the universe, through our guardian divinities and spirits.

✤ 2 ✤

Not one person has ever been born in this world on their own. Birth and growth are all in the hands of God. Everything about a human being occurs through divine assent and will.

✤ 3 ✤

At the moment when you entrust your life, your death and your future wholly to God, your true destiny and heavenly mission will unfold.

✤ 4 ✤

Divine love is always working to make us deeply happy in a fundamental way—apart from our short-term joys or woes. Whatever our short-term outlook may be, let us firmly believe that everything will end well. Let us bide our time with a feeling of gratitude. Such is the way of wise people.

❦ 5 ❧

The only real existence is divinity, which is good, truth and love. Everything else is in the process of fading away.

❦ 6 ❧

Just be true; be true to your divine self.

❦ 7 ❧

Whatever people may seem to be on the surface, their guardian spirits are working for them with all their might. The thing to do is to pray to a person's guardian spirits like this: 'May the person's karma be purified. May their true self come out as soon as possible.' If you do this, both you and the other person will be purified.

❧ 8 ❧

Look up to the sky. Bright energy vibrations are always raining down from heaven.

❧ 9 ❧

The real you, who exists in heaven, is always at work. The only thing you have to do on earth is to keep your mind still and unwavering.

❧ 10 ❧

Make the most of the situation that you are in now.

❧ 11 ❧

Do not get caught up in the past. The past is a vanishing image. It will fade away.

✌ 12 ఌ

Be a good vessel and divine workplace. A good vessel is someone who always attunes themselves to truth, and follows truth.

✌ 13 ఌ

Think this way: 'By working out this problem, I will make one step of progress.' Then, act with an unwavering mind.

✌ 14 ఌ

When we act caring only about our own standpoint, it is called 'egoism.' When we act caring only about another's standpoint, it is called 'love.' When we transcend even love and entrust everything to the divine, it is called *Kuu* or 'Emptiness.'

✌ 15 ఌ

Just before giving us a big job to do, God gives us a job which looks exceedingly trivial at first glance. If we are unaware of this and refuse to do the seemingly trivial job, the arrival of the big job will be delayed considerably. Always keep this in mind.

✒ 16 ✑

A human being's true self is God, who works freely in all directions throughout heaven and earth. Live this and believe it.

✒ 17 ✑

It is certain that the effects of all our past causes will eventually vanish forever. Knowing this is the first step to our spiritual awakening.

✒ 18 ✑

At the moment when you stop attaching yourself to things which are meant to fade away, you will be in oneness with your divine self.

∽ 19 ∾

Whatever you do, you are never doing it by yourself. Everything that you do is the work of the divine universe. Always keep this in mind.

∽ 20 ∾

Whatever may happen around you, and however the situation may look, accept it with thanks, recognizing that nothing appears except through divine love. This is the spirit of faith. Within every occurrence, divine love is revealed and divine mercy can be felt.

∽ 21 ∾

'Thank you for everything. If it is your will to call my life back, even now, just as I am at this moment, I don't mind.' This is the spirit of complete entrustment to the divine.

❧ 22 ❧

The strong point of my teaching is that it helps people to awaken to truth with as little suffering as possible, by adding human affection to divine love.

❧ 23 ❧

There is nothing so noble as an act of sincerity. Whatever fine things a person might say or write, it amounts to nothing unless it is put into action. A person's actions decide everything. One sincere act of truth outweighs the knowledge of a million theories.

❧ 24 ❧

As long as one relies only on one's physical self, there is no hope of attaining wholeness and perfection. One's soul can attain wholeness and perfection only with the help of one's guardian divinities and spirits.

∽ 25 ∾

'God will take good care of this situation for me. My mind is at ease.' To think this way, leaving everything up to divine love, is called 'faith.'

∽ 26 ∾

When you are praying, your true self is shining brightly. If a variety of thoughts pop into your mind it is nothing to worry about, because those thoughts are nothing more than vanishing images from a past consciousness, emerging in order to disappear. Don't be concerned about them at all. Just keep praying.

∽ 27 ∾

If you are unperturbed by the various thoughts that pass through your mind, it means that you have attained perfect serenity, or freedom of mind. But be careful not to mistake euphoria for perfect serenity. Euphoria is a fluctuation of karma, and perfect serenity it the light of your true, divine self, radiating from the depths of your being.

❧ 28 ❧

The great divine wisdom gives us nothing that we do not need. If something seems unnecessary, it only seems that way out of our own immaturity. Everything that occurs is manifested through divine love. All those inconvenient conditions are brought out so they can disappear, dispelling a karmic cause from the past. Recognize this, and rise above what appears on the surface. Look behind those things and discover divine truth. Accept them with thanks, believing that everything happens through merciful divine love.

❧ 29 ❧

Although you may say that you trust in God unconditionally, when something disagreeable happens, you soon become unsettled, doubting divine love. Divine love does not give us bad things. Do not attach yourself to the things which occur around you. Remind yourself that, in the end, everything will turn out for the better, and give thanks.

❧ 30 ❧

Be a tributary of divine love. Do not just receive divine love and let it stop with yourself. Give thanks, then spread the joy to others. The more joy you spread, the more joy will flow to you from God. This is the road which unites us eternally with the divine. This is the fountain of spiritual peace and stability.

❧ 31 ❧

Someone asked Goi Sensei the meaning of 'spiritual awakening.'
His answer was—

Spiritual awakening is being able to feel thankful for everything.

❧ 32 ❧

A free and open mind is best of all. At times, it is a deep ravine where silence is cherished. At other times, it is a rushing torrent of mighty, raging waves. Let your mind be like a river, clear and free-flowing.

∾ 33 ∽

Even though we may reach a high state of spiritual awakenment, if we stop there, we will be unable to rescue others. We need to come down from our lofty tower and be able to live smoothly in unclean surroundings, getting along well with all kinds of people, listening to any kind of talk, and being able to laugh lightheartedly. Unless we can do this, we are only half-awakened.

∾ 34 ∽

If you wish to reach your spiritual awakening, the first thing to do is to let go of fixed ideas. When your head is filled with fixed ideas, whatever else may be poured in, it will all spill out. Let go of pre-existing ideas and listen with an open mind and a straight heart.

∾ 35 ∽

Spiritual awakening is found in the midst of the ordinary. Sincerity, love, acceptance, and appreciation—these qualities are quite ordinary and natural, yet all these are expressions of spiritual awakening.

⤬ 36 ⤬

Very often, a large man-made gem is more beneficial to people than a small authentic gem. In the same way, a person with an expansive personality, even if slightly tarnished, often achieves more than a good or pure person with a narrow outlook. Good people need to become bigger and stronger.

⤬ 37 ⤬

Even though you may physically be in a seated position, your heart, too, needs to be settled down. If your heart is not settled, you will quickly lose composure when you go out into society—into actual daily life. The most important thing is for your heart to sit up straight and never be shaken.

⤬ 38 ⤬

To pray is to let your life shine. Prayer is living life dynamically. If you think that prayer is sitting still without doing anything, there is a misconception somewhere in your idea of prayer.

∽ 39 ∾

When the inner 'you' knows that you are one with the divine, and when the outer 'you' spontaneously performs actions of love at all times, it means that you have reached your spiritual awakening.

∽ 40 ∾

God is expressed only through action.

∽ 41 ∾

Thankfulness is light.

∽ 42 ∾

If you always try to push through your own opinions, you are headed for unhappiness. First, lend an ear to what others are saying. If you do, they will then listen to what you have to say.

∾ 43 ∾

Water flows from the world of our original source. That is why I cherish water.

∾ 44 ∾

People who hide behind their authority, and who oppress the poor and the weak while taking the lion's share for themselves, are in the most loathsome condition of all.

∾ 45 ∾

The state of *Kuu* or 'Emptiness,' in which you leave everything up to the universal law, does not mean that you never cry, never feel sad, or remain uninterested in everything. Just like anyone else, you cry, you feel sad, you laugh, and you joke. But at the same time, your heart is always perfectly clear and cloudless.

৯ 46 ৯

Spiritual faith is not for the purpose of satisfying your desire for reputation or authority. Instead, it is for the purpose of stripping away those kinds of egoistical desires from yourself. In this sense, the path of spiritual faith might be considered painful. But the joy of spiritual faith comes from polishing your character, becoming a better person, and feeling thankful to the universe.

৯ 47 ৯

If you feel like having a good time, go and see a movie or watch TV, but do not join a religion for the sake of amusement. The purpose of religion is to draw out your inner being—your divinity.

৯ 48 ৯

Unless you can transcend the physical vibration and stay within it at the same time, you will be unable to do any real work. When people have achieved a spiritual vibration, they are apt to make light of people who have not done so. If you belittle others or make fun of them in this way, it means that you have lost touch with the true divine spirit. Be very careful not to fall into that trap.

᭥ 49 ᭡

To stay within light without attaching yourself to light, to live in the physical body without attaching yourself to the physical body—this is how I would like for you to be.

᭥ 50 ᭡

One ought to know all about the subconscious, spiritual and divine worlds without being caught up in any of them. At all times, one ought to keep one's physical self directly connected with the infinite self that exists deep within the universal source.

᭥ 51 ᭡

Spirituality does not mean that you say or write fine things. Spirituality must be actually expressed through the body itself. I respect a person who really expresses truth, beauty and harmony in their actions.

✑ 52 ✒

A spiritual leader who lives off the religious offerings of others with a nonchalant, indifferent attitude has hit rock bottom.

✑ 53 ✒

Spiritual leaders ought to be content living in immaculate sparsity. That is the only way of life that spiritual leaders should really care for.

✑ 54 ✒

Human beings need to have 'bigness,' or magnanimity—an all-embracing, generous spirit. Some people are born with this quality, but it can also be developed. Even a single act of thoughtfulness can turn you into a big-hearted person.

∽ 55 ∾

The most dishonorable thing you can do is to use the name of religion to satisfy your selfish cravings.

∽ 56 ∾

Bringing out your true nature is not the same as cultivating psychic or supernatural abilities.

∽ 57 ∾

I acutely feel that it if people would simply do their very best in their own jobs, they would perfect their characters and reach true spiritual awakening more quickly than by undergoing ascetic training or spiritual disciplines.

∽ 58 ∾

If any of you are undergoing spiritual disciplines right now, train yourselves first of all to be humble. Also, reject any kind of spiritual whisperings that may hover around you. Completely reject them, one and all.

◈ 59 ◈

People are not impressed by your words; they are moved by your actions.

◈ 60 ◈

Never try to run from the situation that you are in. If you keep trying to run away from it—telling yourself that this situation is awful and that you really should be somewhere else—the more you struggle to escape, the more you will suffer and the longer your progress will be delayed. There is no better situation for you than the one you are in now. This is because divine love has placed you here, because it is necessary for you to be here.

Accept your situation with gratitude if possible, or accept it grudgingly, but understand that it is necessary. Just make up your mind to apply yourself to your work in all sincerity. If you have a job, do your job to the very best of your ability. If you are a student, give all your effort to your studies. If you do, the way of life that best suits you will come your way. This is what is called making the most of your situation. Later on, you will find that your circumstances have worked for your benefit. There would be no reason for divine love to assign you a task that would not bring you any benefit.

If you steadily pour all your effort into doing your work without resisting it, the moment will come when divine wisdom says 'All right, you have done enough. This phase of your training is over.' Then you will be placed in a new situation or new surroundings. I myself have had that kind of experience in my life.

∽ 61 ∾

The way of spiritual faith is none other than the process of manifesting the divine mind.

∽ 62 ∾

Because you want to accomplish everything in this present lifetime, you rush about and feel stressed. How about looking at it this way: 'I'll take things step by step, and I won't mind if it takes me a few more lifetimes to accomplish what I want to do.'

≪ 63 ≫

No matter how trivial your job may seem to be, you will be given a better job later on if you do your present work with all your heart.

≪ 64 ≫

No matter how meaningless your work might appear to be, think of it as an assignment from the divine will and do it to the best of your ability.

≪ 65 ≫

It sometimes happens that people who do not consider themselves awakened to truth are given brilliant missions. Some of them are accomplishing their mission without being particularly aware of its importance. However, in due time, the mission and the awareness of that kind of person will coincide perfectly, and instantly come into bloom. Therefore, it is a mistake to criticize such people, seeing no further than their superficial appearance.

✆ 66 ✇

Prayer that doesn't become manifest in our actions can't be called true prayer. Prayer makes life come alive. That's what prayer is.

✆ 67 ✇

Prayer is not something that you do by concentrating hard on one point. Prayer is to expand your heart and release your focal point. Rather than holding on to a single objective or thought, you simply return to divine oneness. You merge into oneness with God, and let God take care of everything.

✆ 68 ✇

Do not pamper your karma. Do not compromise with karma. Since God is light, God always delights in a bright, radiant mind.

✒ 69 ✑

What displeases God most is a gloomy expression and a dark frame of mind.

✒ 70 ✑

Suppose you have reached a state of mind where you find yourself content with everything and grateful for everything, whether it is convenient for you or not. That state of mind is called spiritual awakenment.

✒ 71 ✑

Someone asked Goi Sensei: 'What frame of mind should we have when asked to provide people with personal guidance?' His reply was—

Comply with the request while praying for the person's divine missions to be accomplished.

∽ 72 ∾

Don't brood over things. Don't strain yourself by thinking 'I have to uplift people!' Divine love and truth is what uplifts people. The physical being does not have to worry unnecessarily. All the physical being has to do is to live in a relaxed, natural manner.

∽ 73 ∾

If you want to arrange your life as you wish, the first thing to do is to let go of all thoughts.

∽ 74 ∾

Refrain from building up a stockpile of thoughts in your mind.

∽ 75 ∾

People have wondered how it was that my physical body came to be used as a vessel for the divine will. It was because I was gentle, compassionate, and faithful to truth.

From the time I was a child, I always felt that I would rather be hurt myself than hurt other people.

⤙ 76 ⤚

Even if people follow different principles from mine or have a different ideology, I honestly admire their distinguished qualities. That is because greatness of character is separate from principles and ideology.

⤙ 77 ⤚

I really have forgotten what the context was, but Goi Sensei once said to me—

How wonderful it would be if everyone would stop fussing over trifles and nurture an easygoing, big-hearted personality!

⤙ 78 ⤚

Nothing is sillier than predicting what will happen in a certain month of a certain year. People can become obsessed with predictions, whether they are good ones or bad ones.

You will know what happens on that day when that day has actually arrived. It is not good to get turned around and confused by these kinds of predictions, but if you do become confused by them, immerse your confused feelings in the words 'May peace prevail on Earth' and pour all your energy into making your life come alive in your present situation. Make the most of the present. This is the ultimate meaning of spiritual faith.

∽ 79 ∾

It's fine to wish to be useful to others, but you ought to thoroughly reflect on where that feeling comes from. It might just come from a subconscious desire to show off. The useful 'you' and the useless 'you' are both unreal existences—temporary beings that you created yourself. They are in the process of fading away. Freeing yourself from both these unreal beings is your first step toward spiritual awakening.

Just take an unassuming stance and work for others without attracting anyone's notice. Just work brightly, humbly and courageously. When you do, you will become useful to others in a natural way.

≈ 80 ≈

What I consider important is the spontaneous reaction that springs up from your heart. Train yourself so that you can quickly strike out emotions like jealousy, hatred, and dissatisfaction, that pop up all of a sudden.

I have closely observed my own feelings to see what emotions arise, and have found no traces of jealousy, complaint, or dissatisfaction arising at all. I find myself accepting everything with a bright and positive feeling.

Our aim should be to let our true, divine self shine through in any situation, however unexpected. Fear, though, is awfully hard to get rid of. That's why I suggest that you treat all your thoughts and emotions as vanishing images, and cleanse and purify every nook of your subconscious. When you do, your divine light will always shine through, even in unexpected situations.

≈ 81 ≈

I do not like to say nebulous things, such as 'I suppose this will do,' or 'We might make it in time.' I am never satisfied unless I have a clear perspective, and can definitely see that things are going to be all right. I never feel easy unless I am on time, with a little time to spare. When I arrange to meet people, I always allow myself an extra ten or twenty minutes, so that I can arrive a little bit ahead of time.

↭ 82 ↫

To encourage a young girl who was often ill, Goi Sensei said to her—

I, too, go through a lot, and I sometimes suffer. But look at me. I'm always cheerful, aren't I? Do you know why? It is because I know for certain that universal divine love will make everything work out for the better.

↭ 83 ↫

When people around you are ill or in pain, it is not good to strain yourself by thinking 'How terrible!' or 'I must cure them!' It is important to deeply believe that, since the spirit of the universe is love, it never does bad things to people.

When we are meant to live in this world, divine love

keeps us here. When we are meant to go to the next world, divine love sends us there. As for me, I am already beyond the stage of 'believing.' My mind can never be shaken, whatever the circumstances might be. I only emit divine light, that is all. If necessary, I place my hand on a person's forehead, rub their shoulders, or give words of encouragement. But there are also times when I just pray silently and emit light to the person. It all depends on the divine will.

When we entrust everything to the divine will, divine power and light come directly out, right then and there.

❧ 84 ❧

We need to become people who, even if stripped bare of our divine intuition, spiritual abilities, talent, status, and so on, are still left with a wonderful character and personality.

❧ 85 ❧

If you are someone who reflects on your past conduct, it means that you have the special quality of a person of culture.

⋙ 86 ⋘

What the universal will wants is acceptant physical vessels who let its love and light smoothly pass through them without resistance.

⋙ 87 ⋘

All that you, as an individual, have to do is to become a more loving person—to become infinitely warmhearted and thoughtful. Everyone loves to be treated that way. You don't have to be concerned about spiritual power or divine wisdom. Those things come to you from heaven. You only need to become a vessel for receiving them and distributing them to others.

⋙ 88 ⋘

Because bright energy is the existence of God itself, God likes a person to have a bright and sunny mind.

∽ 89 ∾

Please be a deeply thoughtful, gentle, and warmhearted person. Please be one who does not give pain to another's heart. When others simply sit facing you and feel warmth and brightness, even when no words are spoken, then you are the kind of person that I would like for you to be. Even if someone tries to work against you, harm you, or even kill you, it is never all right for you to wound or give pain to their heart. This is because you and others are, in truth, one life and one being.

∽ 90 ∾

At the time when your life first branched out from the original divine light, as a being without a physical body, it had already been decided what kind of work you would do. Your heavenly mission was determined before you were born in this world. So, there is no need to be restless about it. Just keep living life as it comes to you. Just leave everything up to the divine mind.

ৰ্চ 91 ৯ু

The less conscious you are of your individual, physical self, the greater your personality becomes. Your weak self, your good self, and your bad self cease to exist. Neither your good self nor your bad self needs to exist. They are meant to be handed over* to heaven—to the realm of infinite light. All you have to do is melt into that realm, then come back to earth bringing its light with you. In this way, you become transformed into a body of light. The only thing you need to do is to become light.

> * In Japanese, the word for the individual self ('I' or 'me') is pronounced '*watashi*,' and the word for 'hand over' is also pronounced '*watashi*.'

ৰ্চ 92 ৯ু

Do not think of yourself as a mere physical being, but as a divine life. Think that universal love is at work where you are. Feel that divinity is working within you.

❧ 93 ❧

The practice of 'fading away' is not something that you do with your willpower. It is not your physical self that extinguishes karma, or sin. Karma is extinguished by the light of your guardian divinity and spirits. Your part in this process is to pray for world peace.

❧ 94 ❧

In some situations, you cannot help working in the forefront; other times, you have to labor in the background. When you work in the background, you accumulate a store of good deeds—treasures in heaven. If you draw attention to yourself when you are not meant to, you may miss the precious chance to increase your spiritual treasures, and the bright new future that you were creating might fall through in midstream.

❧ 95 ❧

I have often heard people say that they have heard the voice of God, or were given instructions from God. In many cases, these voices or instructions are expressions of the person's subconscious desires. Since it is all but impossible for people to distinguish a divine voice from the voice of their subconscious, what I recommend is that they reject those voices, one and all.

If the messages are true, no matter how hard you deny them, they will naturally appear through your behavior, personality, and daily life. A tree is known by its fruit.

❧ 96 ☙

Psychic perceptions are different from an awakening to truth. Those kinds of perceptions, or abilities, result from disciplines that you went through in past lifetimes. They have nothing to do with the loftiness or baseness of your character. Sometimes, people with psychic perceptions look down on people who do not have such perceptions. They may even delude themselves into thinking that those psychic perceptions prove that they have awakened to truth. Yet one cannot awaken to truth unless one understands that psychic abilities are different from an awakening to truth.

✥ 97 ✥

We shall make a new world—a world without karma. We are now newly building a world made up entirely of light. It is important for you to recognize that the former 'you' does not exist. Think that you are now creating a new human being and a new humanity. Your present suffering has appeared because a wave connected to the past has finally come out, so that it can vanish away.

✥ 98 ✥

Psychic people may tend to become preoccupied with what is going on in the subconscious and spiritual worlds. Because they are so caught up in those worlds, they end up neglecting the physical world they are living in, and this causes problems.

On the other hand, many religious leaders reject the existence of subconscious or spiritual worlds because those worlds are outside the realm of their knowledge or experience. Yet those worlds actually do exist.

I feel that religious leaders should know about the subconscious and spiritual worlds without becoming too preoccupied with them. The most important thing, I think, is for them to guide people to the most fundamental, true world. And to do this, it goes without saying that the leaders themselves have to continually polish their own spirits.

∽ 99 ∾

The fundamental aim of spiritual faith is for people to nourish a free and open mind that is not confined to a fixed framework.

∽ 100 ∾

The best wisdom is supplied to us through prayer.

∽ 101 ∾

When you find yourself in the worst situation, it is a sign that things are going to get better.

❧ 102 ☙

People who practice spiritual faith must never, ever blame others. They need to have big hearts. Forgive yourself and forgive others. Pray for peace with the certainty that all circumstances emerge in the process of fading away.

❧ 103 ☙

Do not attach yourself even to 'good.' Become a person of perfect spiritual freedom.

❧ 104 ☙

When you stay connected with your guardian divinity and spirits, you can intuitively discern good from bad.

❧ 105 ☙

A bright frame of mind is what opens up your destiny.

❦ 106 ❧

What purifies your soul most effectively is to willingly accept even the things that are not pleasant for you. Plunge into them and break through them. The more you try to run away from unpleasant things, they more they chase after you.

❦ 107 ❧

Spiritual faith exists in action. If our actions are not right, we cannot say that we are practicing spiritual faith.

❦ 108 ❧

We are always walking in the midst of God.

❦ 109 ❧

'I come from God.' To live in this firm belief is, itself, prayer.

❧ 110 ❧

Listen to what others are telling you with warm affection, as if they were your own beloved children.

❧ 111 ❧

Do not try to imitate others, and do not rush ahead in haste. Take time and make the best of your own special qualities. Those qualities will come alive in the best and most natural way when you leave everything up to the divine will.

❧ 112 ❧

No matter how hard you try to impress others with words, it won't work. Just fill your heart with love and live naturally, without trying to defend yourself.

❧ 113 ❧

Do not try to analyze yourself too much. All human beings have their strengths and weaknesses. Instead of focusing endlessly on your weak points, try to rapidly expand your strengths. Inner observation is different from self-analysis.

✺ 114 ✺

Trying to make yourself look good by making excuses for everything you do cannot be called fine behavior.

✺ 115 ✺

Let us cultivate big-heartedness. Let us nurture expansive hearts that can accept everything.

✺ 116 ✺

Do not forget the spirit of gratitude, even when things are going well. People tend to forget about gratitude once they have gotten used to their good fortune.

✺ 117 ✺

God is infinite expansiveness. A human is a being who gives expression to the infinite within the scope of the finite.

☙ 118 ❧

Do not adopt any sort of posture in your mind.

☙ 119 ❧

The divine mind is bottomless. There is no point at which we can say, 'Now I have really made it! I don't need to improve any more!' If we think that way, our progress comes to a halt. Let us always, always aim at polishing ourselves to shine more and more brightly.

☙ 120 ❧

Do not form hasty judgments about good and bad based on surface conditions. There have been cases in which large-scale villains have turned into large-scale benefactors overnight. A 'bad person' cannot be labeled as 'bad' through and through.

✧ 121 ✧

Your wholehearted communion with the divine, your continual self-reflection, and your daily faith—these are what save you at critical moments.

✧ 122 ✧

Love of country, or 'patriotism,' does not mean that you care only about bringing profit to your own country. It means that you care about how your country can contribute to the peace and happiness of the world, and that you wish to guide your country in that direction.

✧ 123 ✧

When your thoughts are pure and bright, your life comes alive.

✧ 124 ✧

Human beings cannot become truly happy until their inner mind and their surface consciousness become wholly unified.

∽ 125 ∾

Do not hurl accusations at yourself. Accusations bring you no relief. Once you are able to forgive yourself, you will finally be able to forgive others as well.

∽ 126 ∾

To pray is to lift your consciousness up to the vibrations of spiritual and divine planes.

∽ 127 ∾

If you are involved in the spreading of true principles, you must extinguish your desire for money. You must be able to say, 'No, thank you,' even when you need the money that people are trying to press upon you.

When I was younger, I was sometimes asked to call upon sick people and pray with them. On those occasions, I was often asked to accept money, but I would flatly refuse it and would leave hurriedly, saying, 'No, thank you.' Oftentimes I would later find money in my pocket that someone must have placed there. The universe will definitely provide what you need.

ৰ্ণ 128 ২৯

I do not think that children return even one ten-thousandth of what their parents have done for them. The greatest repayment that you can give to your parents is to contribute to the betterment of society. The returns of this contribution will naturally benefit your parents, your own children, and your children's children, and on through future generations.

ৰ্ণ 129 ২৯

Although you are light, your thoughts reach for darkness. Because you reach for darkness, you are gradually dragged into darkness. You only need to hold yourself steadily within the light, but this may not be easy to do. What I suggest is that you merge with divine light through prayer. Merging with divine light means entering the light of your true self.

◈ 130 ◈

Courage is a priceless treasure.

◈ 131 ◈

Your strengths and your shortcomings exist back to back. If you pour your energy into your shortcomings, trying to correct them, your good qualities will shrink smaller. Instead, pour your energy into your strengths and do your best to expand them. Without your even noticing it, your shortcomings will keep shrinking until they are swallowed up by your strengths. I had shortcomings too, but when I offered up my whole life to the divine will, my strengths alone shone forth and my shortcomings vanished into nothingness. Keep this point in mind, especially when you are offering guidance to others.

◈ 132 ◈

In spiritual faith, your first step is taken when you have transcended the realm of your thoughts.

≪ 133 ≫

When you act, God acts. When you speak, God speaks. The best thing is to just naturally feel that you are one with God.

≪ 134 ≫

Whatever you might be doing, it is not good for your heart to tighten up and get stiff. When you tighten up, it's because you are still thinking that it is your small self that is acting. You stiffen up in direct proportion to the volume of your small self—your ego.

≪ 135 ≫

Human beings are funny. The less great they are, the greater they pretend to be. People who are truly great never try to show how great they are.

∽ 136 ∾

Prayer is not something that you do with tension or strain. Just pray, with an airy feeling, 'May peace prevail on Earth.' Leave everything up to the divine mind, since you know that the physical 'you' can do nothing at all on its own. Just pray, that is all. Entrust everything to divinity with a feeling of thankfulness. Live in prayer without attaching yourself to prayer; live in light without attaching yourself to light.

∽ 137 ∾

Some people think it would be nice if they could see their guardian divinities, hear their voices, or receive detailed instructions from them, but I don't feel that way. I think it's best just to live naturally.

To go through life acting upon detailed instructions voiced by your guardian divinities would not be a true way of life. It would mean that you were not at one with your divine self. You would be separate from God. In that situation, things might go well if you were able to follow the instructions, but if you found yourself unable to do so, you might feel obsessed and intimidated by your guardian divinity, and that would make you lose courage.

If it were absolutely necessary for you to carry out certain divine instructions, you would be able to do so naturally, because your body would spontaneously move that way. The divine will would be reflected in your natural behavior.

You will not become an independent human being until you are ready to take responsibility for your own actions, and make restitution for your own mistakes.

Your real, true way of life as a divine being is discovered when the things that you naturally say and do flow only from your divine self.

৵ 138 ৵

It is of utmost importance for human beings to free themselves from emotionalism. This does not mean that you should repress your emotions, pushing them deeper into your heart. Nor does it mean that you should vent them in front of other people and disturb their peace of mind. What, then, can you do when turbulent emotions rise within you? Pour them into a prayer for world peace, straightaway. Think of all of your negative emotions as being in the process of fading away, and as constantly being transformed into brighter ones through your prayer for world peace. To be able to do this, you need to practice daily.

❧ 139 ❧

I have always been an optimist. No matter what dire straits I was in, I could always look on the bright side. This attitude is what really opened up my path for me.

❧ 140 ❧

I always feel that it is important to peel away spiritual matters and see what kind of person you are in everyday life. None of it has any meaning unless you have a truly good character. Mystical power and wisdom are given from the universe, and the physical person simply receives them with gratitude. What you should do from the physical side is turn your mind to becoming a better person, then thankfully receive the divine wisdom and power that flow to you from heaven.

❧ 141 ❧

Do not seek a dream world from marriage. Marriage is the way in which both parties polish their spirits. It is a golden opportunity for each of them to extinguish their karma.

❧ 142 ❧

You cannot develop your divinity while you are infatuated with yourself.

❧ 143 ❧

In this world, what we need to avoid most is attaching ourselves to something. People attach themselves to a variety of things—money, authority, status, land, or their children—but what lies at the root of all of it is their attachment to their own physical being.

Because people want to gratify their physical being, they attach themselves to things and to people who indulge their karma. But what good does it do to indulge karma? Karma is not even real. It eventually fades away.

Yet people feel pleased when others gratify their karma. They see someone who gratifies their karma as a 'good person' and someone who does not as a 'bad person.'

⤚ 144 ⤙

In general, the distinctions people make between good people and bad people, or likable people and dislikable people, are based on their own emotions. They seldom see a truly good person as good. For them, a good person is someone who serves their interests and a bad person is someone who does not. They gauge everything by their own interests.

As long as people keep thinking this way, the world will never be at peace. But since this kind of attitude is difficult to get rid of, what can people do? I suggest that, at the moment when such feelings emerge, we regard them as being in the process of fading away. All occurrences, feelings, thoughts, and circumstances—good and bad alike—should be directed straight into the waves of a world peace prayer, such as 'Fading away—May peace prevail on Earth.' Within those waves, all things will be purified by the great divine light that is guiding and protecting humanity.

Practice doing this over and over again, and it should give you a clean, sparkly feeling.

⤜ 145 ⤐

For everyone, the world of karma has to be surpassed. Whether they think they have karma or not, all people must transcend the world of their thoughts and reunite with their divine self. So, whenever you speak of the way, or enlighten people through your actions, you need to remind yourself that it is not the physical you who is doing it. It is the divine universe that is doing it.

⤜ 146 ⤐

Courage is what conquers all kinds of karmic thoughts.

⤜ 147 ⤐

I have never guided people with words like: 'Your faith is shallow,' or 'Your dedication is insufficient.' Words like these do not help people. Shallow faith and a lack of dedication are simply the effects of past causes, and pointing them out does no good at all.

Instead, I advise people to cast both their shallow faith and their scanty dedication into a prayer, regarding both as the residue of habitual past thoughts. In the original human nature, there is no such thing as shallow faith or a lack of dedication.

The *you* who is praying now for world peace is directly linked with the divine.

❧ 148 ❧

When you are sad, in pain, or tossed about by violent whirlpools of emotion and cannot pray for world peace, I will be praying for world peace on your behalf. When you cannot give thanks to God, I will be giving thanks to God on your behalf.

❧ 149 ❧

It is indeed true that we are meant to entrust all our thoughts to the light of divine love. Most of us, however, find this very hard to do. That is how the teaching of 'fading away' came about.

What prevent you from entrusting everything to divine love and believing in it completely are the things that you thought in your past lifetimes. Those past thoughts are revealing themselves now because they want to vanish forever. Just tell yourself that this is fading away and release it into the prayer 'May peace prevail on Earth.' It will then be erased by the immense divine light that is guiding the world toward its deliverance.

In writing or in speaking with people, I do not abruptly jump into ultimate truths such as human divinity, human perfection, the non-existence of the physical body, or the non-existence of matter. I first recognize the sin (karma) and helplessness of physical human beings. Based on this recognition, I teach people to have their sins and their helplessness purified in the great light of the world peace prayer.

Teaching human divinity without the practice of 'fading away' could plunge people into a pit of agony—into a restricted state filled with lies and deceit. For most people, I think that the easiest and most natural way to awaken to truth is to fill their hearts with a prayer that carries them out of their helplessness and into the world of their divinity.

≪ 150 ≫

People think of themselves as separate beings, such as 'I,' 'you,' 'he,' and 'she,' but there are no separate physical existences in the true sense. What exist are divine missions, nothing else. Only consciousness exists—the consciousness that strives to attain a mission. So, to become perfectly free, we must transcend all notion of embodiments. Unless we also transcend our preoccupation with our subconscious and spiritual bodies, our consciousness will install itself there and we will cease being free.

Transcend the idea that *you* are your body.

≪ 151 ≫

We are most carefree when we are without consciousness of self.

≪ 152 ≫

All human beings are guided by their guardian spirits and divinities. I am clearly aware of this. You simply may not have observed it. However, there is not much difference between observing it and not observing it. If you believe that all the little details of your daily life are guided by your guardian spirits and divinities, it is the same as if you clearly observed it.

❧ 153 ❧

Even if you have become one with your inner, divine self, it is not the end of the road. Divinity is infinite progress. The state of *Kuu* or 'Emptiness' that you have attained will become deeper and deeper, and your wisdom will increase in radiance.

The way I was in my thirties, just after attaining oneness with my divine self, was different from the way I was in my forties. The way I was after I became one with the five saints* was different from my present self. I make progress from day to day and moment to moment. With each day and each moment, my existence becomes bigger and vaster. I myself don't know how much I will grow in the future. So, there is nothing surprising about other people not being able to understand me.

When people find that they can easily assess themselves, it just means that they do not understand themselves deeply.

* Masahisa Goi's experience of becoming one with five great saints who are working in unison to guide the world to peace is described in his autobiography, *One Who Unites Heaven and Earth*.

❧ 154 ❧

For me, 'bravery' is not even an issue. I neither have bravery nor lack it. My mind is always steady, no matter what. Even in emergencies or moments of crisis, I am always my usual self.

❧ 155 ❧

My prayer is something that can be practiced even while walking or doing things. It is not limited to when you are in a seated position, or have assumed a certain posture in your mind. I am praying right now, as we are talking. Even while I am joking, my mind is always one with God.

❧ 156 ❧

Beauty and harmony are fundamental to spiritual faith. If one does not sense beauty, whether in form or coming from the heart, one cannot truly be called a person of spiritual faith.

❧ 157 ❧

If you have heard disagreeable remarks from someone, do not blame that person for the turmoil you are going through, thinking, for example, 'What an unpleasant person!' Instead, remind yourself that you heard those words because you held a karmic cause for hearing them. Just think that by means of your hearing those words, the karmic causes belonging to you and the other person have been extinguished by that much.

❧ 158 ❧

Your life does not belong to you. It is the divine life of the universe.

◈ 159 ◈

I respect elderly people. There was a poet who said, 'To live is in itself to suffer.' Certainly, it must have been hard at times just to go on living until the age of seventy or eighty. I cannot help but praise them for that.

◈ 160 ◈

Your heart may lose its freedom if you fix your attention too much on one thing. Your mind may lose its openness, and that would show through both in your attitude and in your way of life. It is hard to live fully when your mind is not free.

◈ 161 ◈

What bother me most are excuses. If you cover up your mistakes by saying: 'It couldn't be helped,' or 'It was out of my hands because I left it up to God,' then you are making excuses.

You need not care what other people will think or say. Let them think as they please. Just never make excuses.

God knows everything, so let God deal with people's opinions. Above all, never make excuses to yourself. That is the worst thing you can do because it inhibits your progress.

If you are in the wrong, just apologize to God, saying, 'I am sorry God, I will not do it again.' Since God is your own loving parent, you will surely be forgiven. This is how the principle of 'fading away' takes effect.

It does no good to make excuses, thinking 'It couldn't be helped,' or 'The other party was in the wrong,' or 'I did what anyone would have done.' If you take that standpoint you will never get away from your karma. It will keep on sticking to you.

On the other hand, you can say to yourself: 'It looks as if so-and-so is in the wrong, but I must have had some sort of karmic cause for being treated in that way. Now, our shared karma is being extinguished. May it disappear soon. Thank you, God. May peace prevail on Earth.' This will enable the disharmony to vanish.

There is nothing that 'can't be helped.' Everything happens through the law of cause and effect. So, if someone does something unfavorable to you, it is because, in spite of how well you may have treated the person in this lifetime, you held some sort of karmic cause carried over from a past lifetime.

If you can think, 'Ah, my karma is being erased thanks to this! How grateful I am,' then you have the mind of a Bodhisattva.* It is important for you to become like that.

*A Bodhisattva is a person with a saintly disposition who chooses to be born in this world out of a wish to uplift others.

∞ 162 ∞

Life is working, without a moment's rest. It cannot help but work. So, in order to let your life work freely and smoothly, you must not let your thoughts be shaken. Where, then, can you place your thoughts? Place them within the universal divine mind by praying for world peace. If your thoughts do not pitch and roll, your life will start working more vividly and freely.

∞ 163 ∞

Even if you are not endowed with bravery, courage will rise up from within you as your faith grows deeper.

✂ 164 ✄

Awakened people never think of themselves as great. They just work silently for others. Inconspicuously, in ordinary surroundings, they continue to work for others, whether others esteem them or not. Humble people like these are truly great.

✂ 165 ✄

Suppose 'A' runs a hundred meters in ten seconds and 'B' in eleven seconds. If 'A' says to 'B,' 'I run faster than you,' then 'B' will agree with it. If one's ability is clearly measurable, others will not object to one's taking pride in it.

However, no one can measure your ability in spiritual matters. Even if you say, 'My spirit is high and yours is low,' or 'I am awakened and you are not,' it is nothing more than your own personal opinion.

If you discover a humble feeling within you, it would be fair for you to think that you have made an improvement. But if you find arrogance in your heart, you could safely say that you have slipped down by just that much. This might be your most accurate barometer for assessing yourself.

It is as Jesus once said: 'The meek shall inherit the earth.'

There is a saying that goes: 'Arrogance squelches your talent.' Just as they say, it hurts you to be arrogant.

∽ 166 ∾

To be humble does not mean to belittle yourself. Do not dent your spirit by saying such things as 'I am no good,' or 'I am a hopeless case.' A flat nose may be corrected by plastic surgery, but an excessively dented spirit is not easily corrected. The reason is that in depreciating yourself, you think you are doing a good thing, and others might even agree with you.

I sometimes wonder why people cannot become more frank and straightforward. It is best just to be natural, isn't it?

We are meant to live naturally, making the most of our abilities. You will get tired if you try to exceed your abilities. It all comes back to humility—to steadily do your very best, thinking, 'It is not really enough; I would like to do more.'

The same holds true between husband and wife. The

more devoted you are to each other, the more you appreciate each other, and the more you want to do for each other.

❧ 167 ❧

When you make a show of your own righteousness, it gives others a most disagreeable feeling. Imagine how you would feel if someone projected that kind of attitude, as if to say: 'I am a good person,' 'my faith is unshakable,' 'I am filled with profound love,' and so on. It's not a pleasant spectacle at all.

I do not recommend either arrogance or false humility. I suggest that you just lay your heart bare and live life straightforwardly, thinking 'Thank you God!' and 'It is not my ego that deserves the credit, but God!' If you can always start from this perspective, never losing the spirit of thanks, you will never stagnate or slide backwards.

❧ 168 ❧

Here is a good way to think: 'Day by day, my old self is fading away. Day by day, I am newly reborn, enlivened by divine light from heaven.'

169

Human beings are all flows of light. Each of us is a ray of the one great light. Our bodies do not truly exist. The distinctions between 'I,' 'you,' 'he,' and 'she' exist only temporarily, while we give expression to our divine work.

170

The person who looks so reprehensible is not bad. He or she is just caught up in karma. A person who is thought of as bad is, in fact, carrying out a role of gathering up karma and erasing it on behalf of other people. Think this way: 'It is good of them to have taken the trouble to do that. May their missions be accomplished.' If you can think this way, you are in oneness with your divine self.

171

The world will never become peaceful unless we discard the outworn idea that a human being is a physical body. The point of our peace prayer movement is not to improve the world gradually, but to create an entirely new current of life—a perfectly fresh and new world.

I do not mean to say that a new world will appear suddenly, though. We human beings are going to develop new and better personalities and a fresh approach to life in a perfectly natural way, so that we will look back on our former selves and say 'Goodness, how much I have changed!' without even realizing when it happened.

✦ 172 ✦

Here are three barriers that lie in front of us: a thirst for fame and power, sexual lust, and greediness for material things and money. When feelings like these arise, recognize them and let them be extinguished within a world peace prayer through the light of the divinities. After that, your true mission will open up for you.

✦ 173 ✦

There are people who broadcast their faith saying, 'I am a religious person.' I would like to peel away their religion and see them turn into normal, good-hearted people. A person of narrow perspective who cannot see things that are outside religion cannot really work in this world.

❧ 174 ❧

I can understand parents worrying about their children. It is true that when we have entrusted everything to the divine, there is no need to worry about anything. However, at the same time, it seems to me that because people trust in God, divine love is reflected in them in the form of their caring about their children. Entrusting everything to the divine mind does not mean that there is no need to do anything. This point is easily misunderstood.

❧ 175 ❧

It is important to be content with a life of honest poverty. At the same time, it is also important to have enough grace and composure to feel at home while living in a palace or a castle.

❧ 176 ❧

You do not need to develop a large-scale personality. It is enough to live just as you are within your own capacity, nurturing a pure, bright, gentle, and radiant being.

᭟ 177 ᭠

The teaching about loving your enemies can be difficult to practice. People sometimes find themselves hating even their allies when it is convenient for them to do so. Love is not something that you feel because people have worked for your benefit. The light of your love flows naturally into everyone, even people who said or did something that went against your interests.

᭟ 178 ᭠

I am amazed at the innocent openness of Ryokan-san.* In the process of polishing your heart and improving yourself, it is good to have a person whom you would like to emulate, like Ryokan-san, and to steadily strive toward that goal.

> * Ryokan-san (1758-1831) was a priest who is still widely loved in Japan for his poems and other writings, which are filled with his love for nature, children, and farmers. Refer to #249.

✥ 179 ✥

One can grow as much as one wants to grow. One can improve as much as one wants to improve. That is the wonderful thing about human beings.

✥ 180 ✥

Human beings are mysterious existences. Even though their true being is freely working throughout the universe, their physical self desires to become a certain kind of person. What an interesting thing this is. Perhaps this gives people room for advancement and improvement as human beings. To be born as physical beings, and to move through this world with their physical bodies, gives people a special chance to learn and train themselves step by step.

✥ 181 ✥

Deep in their hearts, all human beings can clearly distinguish good from bad. But to do so, you need to give your full attention to it. If you want to experience something good, do it with your whole being. If you have to experience something bad, hold steady until the very end. When you live this way, you will be able to recognize the truth.

❧ 182 ❧

Let's become people who can bare our hearts before heaven and earth and let our lives resound as clear as a bell. Let's live without any feeling of shame or bashfulness.

❧ 183 ❧

Whether we are doing some kind of important work or not, whether we have accomplished something or not, let's live with the awareness that heaven and earth are completely joined within us. In other words, let's live without leaving any gap at all between our true self and our physical self.

❧ 184 ❧

Pride and arrogance are evidence of silliness. If someone says, 'I am great,' you can interpret that as meaning that he or she is the silliest person around. Similarly, if someone brags about being enlightened, you can take that to mean that the person is not enlightened.

∻ 185 ∻

Just because you tell people to become more open and acceptant of truth, it does not mean that they will be able to do it. Those who can are people who were born with this ability. Qualities like acceptance of truth, gentleness, brightness, and courage derive not from one's present consciousness, but from experiences that one had in past lifetimes.

When we think about this, we can make up our minds to spend our present lifetime settling our spiritual debts from the past—which is what I call 'fading away'—while at the same time building up our spiritual savings for the future. So, no matter how much pain and agony you might have had in this life, in the long run it is not so considerable. Keep your thoughts pure and clean; let your true mind shine, no matter how miserable your circumstances are. This is of great importance.

❦ 186 ❧

The greatest talent we can have in this world is a talent for revealing the hidden wonders of the universe and the truth, goodness, and beauty of life.

❦ 187 ❧

Some people say, 'That was my fate,' or 'This is my destiny' at every opportunity, and many feel powerless in face of their fate. Actually, one's self and one's fate are two different things. Your fate is not your present self. It is a manifestation of what you thought and did before. It is showing itself now while in the process of vanishing away. It is disappearing now in front of your eyes. So, even if your fate and your circumstances seem bad, this does not mean that you are bad now. And for the same reason, even if your fate is splendid, it is not because you are good and great now.

If your circumstances are harsh or unpleasant, do not grieve over them, blame yourself, or feel ashamed of your present self. And if you feel that your circumstances are good, just be grateful for them without being prideful or conceited.

If things like these are just fading away, where, then, is the 'you' of the present? It exists within the great divine mind. Your present self is one ray of the infinite life of the universe, holding its own unique character. All the conditions that appear in front of this infinite self are in the process of fading away.

If you consistently believe this, you will no longer be annoyed by fears or worries about life and death, and you will develop an unwavering spirit that comprehends the eternity of your life.

◈ 188 ◈

Everyone has to walk through a deep canyon once in their life. If you fear the difficulty that awaits you there, and try to run away from it, your future will never open up for you. You could think of it as if you were walking through a muddy patch in the road—the more you try to circumvent it in fear of getting dirty, the more soiled you become.

Since going through this muddy patch is the only way you can get to your destination, just walk ahead without being afraid of the mud. Just move forward and do not run away, because beyond this muddy patch lies a beautiful and level path.

❧ 189 ❧

Your future is bound to improve if you hold firm through the deepest part of your anguish. To do this, you need to believe in divine love. Divine love never gives you pain that you cannot endure. But if you feel that your pain is too much for you, come to see me. You can join a meditation gathering, listen to my talks, or hear my whistling and hand-clapping.* Before you know it, your inner courage and brightness will naturally well up, enabling you to overcome your difficulty.

When you are faced with a misfortune, do not view it only as a misfortune. It is important to have the kind of faith that strengthens and elevates you, so that you can recognize any problem as the now-disappearing effect of a past karmic cause, and take it as a sign that things are definitely going to get better. To develop this kind of faith, intently practice the method of 'Fading away—May peace prevail on Earth.' This will allow your guardian divinities and spirits—along with the great divine light of global deliverance—to uplift your mental state before you are even aware of it.

* During guided meditation, Goi Sensei used to clap his hands together in a purifying way, and he sometimes emitted a gentle whistling sound. Nowadays these sounds can be heard on tape.

❦ 190 ❦

If you are looking for a way to assist someone who is in a difficult situation, you can offer support to the person's guardian spirits in this way: 'May the person's karma vanish away a little sooner, and may their true self shine through. Please love them; please help them. May peace prevail on Earth.'

❦ 191 ❦

The very worst times are also the times when your future opens up.

❦ 192 ❦

It is important to be bright and expansive. It is not good to blame yourself too much. Do what you want to do with dignity and confidence. If it ends in failure, let it fade away.

Start all your actions with a prayerful feeling, and do not spend too much time mulling over whether you did well or did badly. Be big-hearted, be at ease, and let your life flow.

≪⁓ 193 ⁓≫

The fundamental aim of spiritual faith is to rise above our physical consciousness. We need to throw away the idea that our physical being is doing everything. If we think that our physical self is doing the work, it is not spiritual faith but self-discipline. When you feel the necessity to become a certain way or achieve certain results, that is also self-discipline.

Spiritual faith, on the other hand, means to re-enter our divine source, the divine mind of the universe. The 'you' that appears physically is not really a physical individual, but a branching out of divine life—a ray of the one great, bright, universal light, appearing in this world because it has work to do.

Your physical consciousness does not have to make the world peaceful, nor does it have to awaken itself. All that your physical consciousness needs to do is to enter the great divine light through prayer for world peace. This is the most important thing to do.

Afterward, you will find that out of that great light, your true self, which existed long before your physical body did, is revealing itself now through your physical being. Therefore, all you need to do from the physical side is to 'flick the switch' for entering the divine mind. This is what I call 'complete entrustment.'

≪ 194 ≫

So long as you regard your individual self, identified by your name, as the real 'you,' you inevitably attach yourself to the habits and way of life that relate to your individual being. In doing so, you prevent the source of your life from flowing through smoothly. Instead, regard your individual habits as fading away. Immerse them in the great light of a world peace prayer while thinking that a ray of great divine light is flowing where you are. When you think and feel this way, you can lead your life in a composed and carefree manner.

≪ 195 ≫

When you are beginning to feel your divine awareness, you might sometimes wonder what you would do if it suddenly disappeared in midstream. Or, you might feel nervous about what you should do if your consciousness wandered off somewhere during meditation and never returned. Or, you might feel apprehensive about what would happen if your mind went blank while you were speaking about truth, and you could not go on with what you were saying. Rest assured that those things will never happen. Your consciousness will never get lost, and if your mind goes blank for a second, it will indeed return to normal and you will be able to finish what you were saying.

Just relax and live with confidence, believing that your divinely given missions will surely be accomplished.

∽ 196 ∾

The most important frame of mind for us to have is love, or what we call 'the spirit of selflessness.' In other words, it is to find joy purely in pleasing another's true self by drawing out his or her wonderful qualities.

∽ 197 ∾

Human beings find it hard to love when things are not going their way, and sometimes they even hate others instead. They are able to love only when all is going well for them. But unless you can love consistently, regardless of whether conditions are favorable or unfavorable, your love is not genuine.

⋘ 198 ⋙

If you keep thinking of others all the time, the caring thoughts that you send out will come back to you.

⋘ 199 ⋙

The practice of 'fading away' is something that you do in your own life. It is not meant to be forced on others.

⋘ 200 ⋙

The best way to live is by making the most of your own special qualities. In this way you steadily become a better and better person.

201

I would like people to be ordinary, yet nice—humble, yet radiant. I would like them to express their shining, inner selves and become people of deep love.

I am not interested in training people to become ascetics. Even if someone knows their way around the subconscious world, what good does that do? It is quite unnecessary. What I most wish is for people to be able to let all their words and actions overflow with love and sincerity.

202

Do not sermonize through your mouth; express truth through your body.

203

Being overzealous is dangerous. When I was young, I had some overzealous tendencies, so I know through experience how dangerous it is. One false step can bring ruin to yourself and the people working with you. Yet up until now, unless people had a great deal of enthusiasm, they could not achieve what they were aiming for.

But those times are over. From now on, over-enthusiasm simply will not do. The only way to proceed is with an honest, sober, steady, and tranquil peace movement. Otherwise, no real work will be done. The people at the center must be free from personal ambition and greed. However, it is not easy to be that way. In spiritual groups, there is almost always some sort of desire for authority, and that is very hard to get rid of.

Some might protest, saying 'No, not me!' And perhaps they do not show any personal greed. Instead, the object of their selfishness shifts to the movement that they are volunteering for, so that they end up denouncing other groups, or contriving to defeat them. This is why you need to keep a cool head and carefully observe yourself and your actions.

◈ 204 ◈

If this Earth perishes, how can you build your own future and the future happiness of your family?

The visible world and the invisible world are brimming over with conditions that could destroy the Earth, not only through wars, but also through calamities and natural disasters.

Right now, we must live wholly within the spirit of prayer for world peace. If you want your own way, if you want to amuse yourself, if you want to be greedy, set these things aside for another day. Now—right now—pray, and pray, and pray for world peace.

Prayer is not seen with the eyes. That is why people who have awakened to their spirituality must go first, filling every corner of their life with prayer. Through their actions, their way of life, and their personality, others will awaken, too.

❧ 205 ❧

If you go and train in the mountains, sit under waterfalls, and spend long hours in seated meditation, it may be hard in a physical sense. But to me, that kind of training seems fairly easy, because you went there with that purpose in mind, and you have nothing but that to do. In the mental or spiritual sense, it is not so very taxing.

On the other hand, if you live in the city and are tied down with matters of everyday life, it is a different story. You never know what is going to happen, or when. In that situation, it is much more difficult to practice oneness with your divine self.

People in the old days had a very good saying: 'A great saint is born from the town.' It is so, just as they said.

❧ 206 ❧

I do not ask people to rid themselves of their thoughts. I know how difficult that is. Instead, I ask them to redirect their thoughts. The best way to redirect your thoughts, I feel, is to pray for world peace.

❧ 207 ❧

You need not care about each and every word that others say. Be faithful only to your divine self.

❧ 208 ❧

As things occur around you, if you think: 'It has vanished! It is gone!' it is the same as letting your inner divine nature shine forth.

∽ 209 ∾

Eventually, the physical body has to die. But while your physical body lives, you must live, too. Since you must live, live wholeheartedly.

∽ 210 ∾

Think only bright thoughts. God rejoices in a sunny mind.

∽ 211 ∾

There are times when your life comes alive—when you are longing for the happiness of others, when you are working for the good of others, when you are searching for your true self, when you are striving to accomplish your divine purpose in this world. But, oh, how very many people in this world are 'living dead people.'

∽ 212 ∾

Always look upon others as you would look upon God. Always treat others as you would treat God.

❧ 213 ❧

Christ is not the only Christ. Buddha is not the only Buddha. Everyone's true nature is Christ. Everyone's true nature is Buddha.

❧ 214 ❧

Even if you do something good, it does not become a truly good deed if there is 'self' in your action. You have to outgrow the 'shell' or 'boundary' that you built around yourself.

❧ 215 ❧

Look at yourself closely. The pure, serene you is the real you. The soiled things, the murky things, the uneasy or unsteady things are clouds passing in front of the real you.

❧ 216 ❧

Do not be a hypocrite. Do not pretend to be either good or bad. Unmask yourself and let people see you as you are.

Say that this is how you are, no more and no less, and that you are striving to do better.

≪ 217 ≫

It is not good to pretend to be something you are not, nor is it good to imitate someone else. Simply let your own natural qualities show through, just as they are.

≪ 218 ≫

To be free from karma, focus only on your inner light.

≪ 219 ≫

You cannot serve as a guide for others unless you have the disposition of an ordinary person.

≪ 220 ≫

Whatever may haunt you, it will naturally vanish when you pray for world peace, praise God, and become truly unified with your guardian spirits and divinities.

❧ 221 ❧

Even if you think that your intuition may be coming from your guardian spirits, if your thoughts are negative and your words could bring fear to others, you must reject those intuitive feelings.

❧ 222 ❧

Your physical being is a vessel that is utilized by the divine will. When you are empty of all thoughts, the divine will can flow through your mind.

❧ 223 ❧

To reach the state of *Kuu*, or 'Emptiness,' entrust everything to your guardian divinities and spirits.

❧ 224 ❧

Thankfulness is leaving everything up to the love of the universe.

❧ 225 ❧

When divine love acts upon you, it is always through your guardian divinities and spirits.

❧ 226 ❧

A person's true greatness is always discerned though their actions. No matter what marvelous theories they may expound, no matter what fabulous psychic powers they may possess, if their actions are without love, we cannot say that the person is a saint.

❧ 227 ❧

If something undesirable should surface, think intently: 'My karma from the past has vanished through this. Things will absolutely get better from now on.'

❧ 228 ❧

Our greatest happiness is when we are unified, heart and soul, with the divine mind.

✺ 229 ✺

Anxiety and anguish accumulate in the body as poison, but your inner life-power expels it in the form of diarrhea or phlegm.

✺ 230 ✺

The life within you is God. To use the power of life wastefully is blasphemy against God.

✺ 231 ✺

To melt into the divine with heartfelt thankfulness—this is prayer.

✺ 232 ✺

Rapidly expand your good qualities without pondering your shortcomings. Live with dignity and composure.

❧ 233 ❧

You are always in a party of two: yourself and God.

❧ 234 ❧

People come to religion seeking peace of mind. Therefore, if a religion fosters fear, it is a mistaken religion.

❧ 235 ❧

When you leave everything up to universal love, anxiety disappears and you gain extra space in your mind. You also gain extra capacity in your time. You are able to do large jobs in a short time, and accomplish many times more work than you thought you could do.

❧ 236 ❧

The spirit of faith is love, sincerity, and beauty. You do not necessarily have to belong to a religious group. Simply let this spirit come alive.

✥ 237 ✥

Just be ordinary. There is no need to aim at being extraordinary.

✥ 238 ✥

While living an average, ordinary life, try to let warmth, serenity, and happiness radiate from your whole being.

✥ 239 ✥

A prayer of love spurs people into action.

✥ 240 ✥

Happy are those who can steadily continue loving one person. No one is unhappier than those who cannot truly love one person, and cannot love a lot of people either. There are some who are capable of loving a great many people, yet can also love each of them individually with their whole heart. Such people could be thought of as saints.

✑ 241 ✑

It is not so difficult to live in such a way that you kill small insects and let the big ones live. What is difficult is to live in such a way that you let both the small and the big insects live.

The way of life in which you weed out the unpromising ones and let the promising ones develop is not so difficult. What is difficult is to bring out the best in the promising ones and the unpromising ones as well.

✑ 242 ✑

There are many sad things in our life. However, we unexpectedly find that underneath those sad things, a bright light is shining.

✑ 243 ✑

Human beings must be true to God. At the same time, we must be true to ourselves. Do not deceive yourself, and bare your soul before God.

If a bad 'self' appears—a 'self' that you are embarrassed for God to see—it is the vanishing image of a thought from the past that had been apart from the divine mind. It has emerged now so that it can fade away upon being immersed in divine light. Hand such thoughts over to the divine will, along with a prayer for world peace. Apologize to heaven and ask that your soul may be purified in its perfect, divine light.

❦ 244 ❦

Your soul is set free when you know that, no matter how great the pain, any and all suffering will absolutely vanish with the passing of time.

❦ 245 ❦

As long as you keep holding on to the circumstances, thoughts, and feelings that appear—and keep trying to discern which are good and which are bad—you will not know peace of mind.

❦ 246 ❧

Whatever the circumstances, actions that maintain a peaceful, bright, and upright state of mind will carve out a bright future for you.

❦ 247 ❧

Someone who has mastered an art usually does not talk much about it. If you meet someone who boasts about whatever it is that they do, it is likely that they are still not very well versed in it.

❦ 248 ❧

You can mend your own ways by seeing how others behave. There is a lot you can learn from observing what other people do. When you observe a mistaken attitude or mistaken behavior in someone, you can say to yourself: 'I don't want to be that way,' or 'I don't want to make the same mistake.' Similarly, if you observe actions worth emulating, you can tell yourself: 'Oh, I want to be like that person!'

⊰ 249 ⊱

I am not sure how this subject came up, but Goi Sensei once commented—

Ryokan was a great priest! Thrown overboard by the skipper of a boat, he suddenly found himself in the middle of the sea, floating and sinking alternately at the mercy of the waves. Leaving his fate to the divine will, he remained in a calm state as he bobbed up and down in the water. Unnerved by the priest's composure, the skipper, who had thrown him into the water intentionally, pulled Ryokan out of the sea. Upon doing so, the skipper was met with profuse thanks and praise from the priest, who put his hands together exclaiming, 'You saved my life! Thank you!'

This story makes us feel truly humble. It is not easy to calmly let your fate take its course when you are unexpectedly thrown into life-threatening circumstances. In such moments, a person's true feelings come out. If you feel alarmed in such situations, you know that you still have many lessons to learn.

Kurozumi Munetada* offers us a good example of this. One day, on his way to give a talk, he had to cross a bridge made of logs. As he started across, he lost his balance as the bridge lurched from side to side, and he cried out in alarm. When he got to the other side, he sat down on the river bank, raised his eyes to heaven, and apologized to God, saying 'Heavenly Mother, forgive me for disturbing your divine composure.' And the story goes that, in front of all of those present, he exclaimed, 'I still have many lessons to learn!'

In spoken words and in writing, we can say anything we like, but the important thing is to put those ideas into practice. It takes enormous effort to transform our words into actions, but we must keep practicing until we can act instantly.

The stories of Ryokan and Kurozumi give us good examples, don't they!

* Kurozumi Munetada (1780-1850) was the founder of a sect of Shintoism.

250

Anyone who has been held at gunpoint, or crossed a wobbly bridge of logs, must certainly have experienced a breathtaking moment of fear. In such situations, people who are in the habit of praying the world peace prayer would probably lose no time in praying 'Fading away—May peace prevail on Earth,' or in thinking of my teachings. At any rate, even if alarmed momentarily, they would soon regain their composure.

To go one step further, I would like to cite an instance when Saigo Nanshu* maintained his calm as lightening struck just next to him. A firm believer in his own destiny, he accepted that he would die when his time to die came, and he did not flinch in the least when a lightening bolt struck within inches of him. I would like to see all of you become like this, always maintaining your normal composure, so that your spirits never waver or flinch. This will occur naturally as your prayers become deeper.

* Saigo Nanshu, a central figure in Japanese history, is highly respected for his role in establishing a new government without bloodshed at the start of the Meiji era, about 160 years ago.

❦ 251 ❦

Your physical body is here on earth in order to fill this world with the light of your original being. What is blocking the light is the thought that you are merely your physical self. Once that thought vanishes, your original divine light will shine. This is because all of us are essentially divine beings.

◆ 252 ◆

Even without thinking of making your existence known, your light will come through when you gracefully accept the situation you are in. Trying too hard, or being excessively preoccupied with various circumstances, will hinder the light. With child-like simplicity, entrust yourself wholly to the universal will in a gentle and flexible way. Your way of living will shine as you go about life in the usual way.

◆ 253 ◆

Thoughts of gratitude are light.

◆ 254 ◆

We shed many kinds of tears. There are tears of sorrow, and tears of worldly happiness. But tears of joy and thankfulness which come from the soul are light.

∽ 255 ∾

A person's small weaknesses endear that person to us even more.

∽ 256 ∾

Never believe in rumors.

∽ 257 ∾

If you call to the divine mind with all your heart, it will surely come to you. But never call upon God with feelings of denial, such as: 'It's no use calling on God,' or 'God would never come to someone like me.' If feelings like these emerge, reject them right away by thinking that they are in the process of vanishing. When you do this, God will come straight to you.

∽ 258 ∾

Act in earnest, and never lose the extra space that you have in your mind.

❧ 259 ❧

Beauty is a resonance that precedes sensation. Among the divine qualities of truth, goodness, and beauty, beauty is at the apex. Beauty is the expression of the divine mind, the manifestation of love and harmony.

❧ 260 ❧

All things beautiful are the resonance of divine life.

❧ 261 ❧

When things seem to be at their worst, and beyond our control, that is the time when the dawn is nearest. It is a sign that good things will certainly come.

❧ 262 ❧

The greater your suffering and the deeper your pain, the greater and deeper will be the joy that follows.

⇜ 263 ⇝

Whether we receive gratitude for it or not, whether we stand out in a crowd or not, let's do our utmost for others. Secret acts of love are precious treasures. They are gems that are collected and stored in heaven.

⇜ 264 ⇝

The kind of person who does not feel alarmed in the least, even if they become poor, or ill, or whatever else might happen; the kind of person who might falter for an instant, but quickly realizes that this is fading away, and returns to wholehearted prayer—my job is to assist everyone in becoming this kind of person.

⇜ 265 ⇝

Someone who never feels frightened, no matter what happens; someone who never hates, no matter what happens; someone whose heart overflows with love, no matter what happens—this is the kind of person I would like for you to be.

✒ 266 ✑

Learn to listen with your heart to what others have to say. This is perhaps an important condition for becoming a person of great character.

✒ 267 ✑

Let us become big-hearted, easygoing, warm human beings.

✒ 268 ✑

Whether this world becomes a better place depends on whether each individual becomes a better person.

✒ 269 ✑

Although have something wonderful that shines brightly within us, it goes unnoticed by ourselves and others, because it has been thickly veiled by the thought-habits that we have built up over a long, long period of time. Yet sometimes, as if by chance, our inner splendor suddenly reveals itself for all to see.

That's why we must never ridicule anyone or make light of their potential, whether it is a child, or a grownup, or whoever it may be. We never know how great the person may turn out to be. Keep in mind that there are times when even the most hardened criminal turns into a holy person.

✆ 270 ❧

Goi Sensei handed someone a piece of paper on which were written the words 'A way to cure illness.' The instructions went like this—

Whatever thoughts might spring to mind, convert all of them to the words 'Thank you, God.' If you keep doing this, your illness will be cured.

✆ 271 ❧

It says in the Bible that not everyone who cries 'Lord! Lord!' will enter the gates of heaven, and this is indeed true. No matter how often a person may call out the name of God, if their actions are less than average, there is nothing special we can say about them. Unless you have a lot of love in your heart, whatever your talents may be, they will not really come alive. The first thing to do is to become a gentle-hearted person.

∽ 272 ∾

To call oneself 'great,' one would have to be extremely silly. There is no point in comparing people to each other to see who is great and who is not, because there is little difference among human beings from the viewpoint of heaven. It is like viewing the Earth from space. From that perspective, there is little difference between low-lying hills and the peaks of the Himalayas.

∽ 273 ∾

Think of your body as a vessel which divine light passes through. If someone is ill, and you think that you must cure them, only your limited, physical power can come through. It is not necessary to wonder whether you can heal someone or not. This has nothing to do with being weak-willed or strong-willed, educated or uneducated, experienced or inexperienced. You become strong when you think of nothing, and only pray: 'Please let me be an instrument for divine light to shine through.'

❧ 274 ❧

If you want to make the world a better place, your first step is to live wholly and completely in the spirit of prayer.

❧ 275 ❧

The highest of good deeds are done in secret. The lowest ones are done in an effort to make a good name for oneself.

❧ 276 ❧

When I see people who pray to God, yet torment or bully others, it gives me a very disagreeable feeling. If that is how they practice their faith, it would be better for them to give up on their religious path and put all their effort into making a good living and providing for their families. Things like that come before religion.

❦ 277 ❧

From time to time, you might feel that you have had a pre-monition about something. Some people become agitated when they feel that they have had a foreboding feeling about going somewhere, and they fret over whether or not they should go. To my mind, this is a silly thing to do. If they were truly meant not to go somewhere, the divine will would arrange for them not to go. It is not a matter of premonitions. It simply means that the situation has become such that they should not go. The divine will works at a level far deeper than premonitions.

It is enough to just live naturally, I think. If you cannot go somewhere, it is best that you do not go. If you cannot meet a certain person, it is best that you do not meet them. Being able to acknowledge and forgive everything, with the understanding that all things and all occurrences have their own meaning and purpose, is perhaps what 'enlightenment' is about. As the philosopher Lao Tsu taught us, 'Act in no-action,'* and do your best at your own job. If you are a salaried person, go to your office and pour all of your energy into your daily work. If you are a tradesperson, work hard at your trade.

* Elsewhere, Masahisa Goi writes: 'The true Sage always acts as a vessel for the universal divine law. Never does he or she act upon the orders of the physical brain. This is how one acts in No-action.' (from *The Spirit of Lao Tsu*, Masahisa Goi, Byakko Press, 2001)

ৰ্ক 278 ৯০

Without standing under cold waterfalls or secluding yourself in the mountains, you can find a place close by where there are more challenging ascetic practices. This ascetic training ground is called family life. People's karma often collides with the karma of those who are close to them. When this happens, if you can smoothly neutralize the karma without hurting yourself or others, and bring about harmony in your family, it means that you are a fine, full-fledged human being, and this quality will stay with you wherever you may go.

ৰ্ক 279 ৯০

I once approached Goi Sensei to let him know that the president of a certain company wanted him to deliver a motivating speech to his staff, but Goi Sensei promptly declined the invitation, saying—

There is nothing less effective than just giving people sermons. No one listens to them. As the Bible says, *Ask, and it shall be given you; seek, and ye shall find; knock, and it shall be opened unto you* (Luke 11:9), but to give speeches to people who did not ask for them is a waste of time.

Even if the chief of a company is kind to the staff, if she (or he) does not show generosity in material terms, the prevailing attitude will be, 'Our boss is nice enough, but stingy. We can't buy anything with her nice manners.' On the other hand, even if the chief is demanding and sometimes gets cross with her staff, if she provides for them generously, the staff will feel, 'Our boss can be rather demanding at times, but at least we can talk with her.' If you are the president of a company, or occupy that kind of position, you ought to be able to inspire your staff with your presidential qualities. When you stand before them, you should be able to instill in them the desire to work hard. As time goes on, those qualities should start to emanate from your presence.

❧ 280 ❧

Divine truth is apportioned to all people equally. If you become the founder of a religion or the president of a company, that was determined by your light-filled actions during a previous lifetime. It would be nice if we could say that a person's high position in this world corresponds perfectly with the height of their spirituality, but this is generally not the case. For example, let's say that a certain person teaches people a wonderful, true principle, and many people are uplifted by it. Even so, that in itself is not an indication of the teacher's own degree of awakening. At all times, one's spiritual state is demonstrated through one's thoughts and actions. If one's words are not consistent with one's actions, we cannot say that one is living as an awakened person.

The first step to our awakening is made when we have risen above emotionalism.

❧ 281 ❧

Never make fun of anyone. You have no idea of the wonderful qualities that lie hidden within that person.

✌ 282 ✍

Do you know how to turn a trembling heart into a strong one? Always tell yourself firmly: 'My guardian spirits are with me at all times, and they are making everything work out for the better. Thank you, guardian spirits!'

✌ 283 ✍

If the reason you decided to join a religious group was that you were afraid to go to school, or did not want to work within society, you may end up cutting yourself off from the down-to-earth feeling of living in society. Do not run away from things that you find unpleasant. Rather, start by dealing with the very things that are unpleasant for you. The divine mind lives within you, so call upon your divinity as you grapple earnestly with your difficulties. The cloud of fear or depression that haunts you will lift in an instant.

❧ 284 ❧

Do your best at the tasks before you, even those that seem tedious or insignificant. This is the way of living that makes our peace movement come alive.

❧ 285 ❧

'How I envy him! How I wish I were in her shoes!' These kinds of thoughts defeat the spirits of many people. They think they cannot achieve their dreams because they lack the right environment or talents. These people ought to stop and take an honest look at their own hearts and their own surroundings.

❧ 286 ❧

In our society, we have many types of people doing many types of things. All these people have their strengths and their weaknesses. Yet, if there are even a few people working for the peace and happiness of humanity, shouldn't we overlook their faults and admire them for their strengths? To work for the happiness of others, and to live for the sake of others—isn't that in itself a praiseworthy thing?

∽ 287 ∾

There is a proverb that says too much thinking will get you nowhere, and this applies to religion, too. Those who get too involved in religion can be difficult to deal with. They cannot live in harmony with the rest of the world. Those who cannot live harmoniously with other people are like dropouts from society. I would like for you to become people who can handle the matters of this world in the usual way, and at the same time, hold something exceptionally wonderful within you.

∽ 288 ∾

Life that shines out healthily is beautiful. Think about a baby, for example. A baby lives life naturally, just as it comes. That is why a baby is cute. When we see it, our feelings are lightened and softened. It is good to live life naturally, just as it comes.

❧ 289 ❧

Spiritual faith means leaving everything up to divine love. Nothing else needs to be added.

It would be good if you could accept everything that happens around you, thinking, 'It's all right. There is a divine meaning underneath it.' This, however, may not be easy to do. So instead, just think that everything, whether good or bad, is fading away, and keep thinking or praying, 'May peace prevail on Earth.' Do this all the time, with your whole being. There is no substitute for steady practice.

❧ 290 ❧

Some people tire themselves out because they worry too much about what others think. Those people need to toughen up a little. They should not care about what others may think or say. This frame of mind is just right for a good-tempered, gentle-minded person.

∽ 291 ∾

I cannot hold myself aloof from everything, saying that what happens to others doesn't concern me because it is the divine will. If I see someone who is ill, or in financial difficulty, I feel concerned about them—even to the point of worrying about how much money they might have in their wallet. But this does not mean that I drown myself in pity or anxiety. I always feel that through my feelings of compassion or concern, the light of divine love naturally flows into the person and permeates their heart.

There are some who appear to treat others indifferently, yet truly love them and assist them in making the most of their life. There are others who appear to be enlightened, yet actually have cold hearts. Still others seem to be overly emotional and to indulge in excesses of compassion, yet in reality they are not as they seem. There are many, many kinds of people, and it is no easy matter to draw a line between love and emotionalism.

In truth, however, all human beings possess the ability to tell the difference.

∾ 292 ∾

A heart that can smoothly accept truth is a treasure indeed.

∾ 293 ∾

Start by tackling the jobs that you are not fond of doing.

∾ 294 ∾

Your guardian divinities and spirits are your awakened spiritual ancestors. They are your own dear grandmothers and grandfathers.

∾ 295 ∾

Your guardian divinities and spirits are always with you. They are at one with you. They are your own divine angels.

✥ 296 ❧

Various angelic beings who assist and guide you may sometimes go away, but your own guardian spirits never leave you, not even for a moment. Whatever the time, whatever the situation, they are always watching over you and protecting you.

✥ 297 ❧

Your guardian divinities and spirits are always keeping a close watch on the movements of your heart.

✥ 298 ❧

War debases human beings to a level beneath that of animals. Hatred paralyzes their conscience, so that they feel no shame in performing cruel acts on a wide scale.

At all times and in all situations, human beings must nurture a heart free from all hatred and resentment—a heart filled with peace.

∽ 299 ∾

In many cases, people who enter a spiritual path tend to be timid. But whether timid or willful, they all have their egos. Once they lose their egos by immersing themselves in the great divine light of the world peace prayer, there is no longer any such thing as timidity or willfulness.

∽ 300 ∾

You cannot be called a leader until your heart is not shaken by anything and does not attach itself to anything.

∽ 301 ∾

If you have committed three wrongs, firmly make up your mind that you will not do the same things again, then do five or six good things with a good, strong will. If you do this, the balance will be two or three points on the positive side.

It is foolish to always dwell on your mistakes.

∽ 302 ∾

The spirit of faith is the spirit of service. Making others happy comes before personal pleasure. Comforting others comes before your personal suffering. If you are not able to take a humble position, it cannot be said that you have the spirit of faith.

∽ 303 ∾

Making the most of life means to willingly accept the work that has been assigned to you, and to do it to the best of your ability in whatever place you happen to be.

Divinity becomes manifest through two aspects: action and prayer.

∽ 304 ∾

If someone says something to you that makes you feel uncomfortable, think that the person truly cares about you. A person who truly loves you does not give you only sweet words.

✑ 305 ✐

Here is what Goi Sensei said to me when I told him about the fear I experienced when I stayed overnight at Holy Hill.*

Fear presents itself in human hearts when we encounter a strong divine light. This happened to me several times while I was undergoing my own spiritual training.** What I would do at those times was to emit a silent shout in my mind. When I did that, my fear would disappear. At such times, it does not help to turn your thoughts to other things. If you like, you could even shout out loud. Just shout, with all your might. Your fear will evaporate. You will see.

When you felt afraid, your guardian divinity had brought you in touch with a strong divine light in order to draw out and extinguish the fear and other unnecessary emotions that were stored within you. From now on, you will be stronger than before. That's good, isn't it!

When all is said and done, the best practice is to entrust yourself wholly to the divine mind. You will live in this world as long as you have a mission here to fulfill, and you will leave this world when there is nothing more that you must do. Believe this through and through.

* Holy Hill refers to a prayer center located in Ichikawa, Japan from the 1950s until 1999.

** For details about Masahisa Goi's spiritual training, refer to his autobiography, *One Who Unites Heaven and Earth*.

ᏸ 306 ᏸ

Love is proportionate to the depth of one's patience.

ᏸ 307 ᏸ

Do not try to run away from pain and sorrow. The harder you try to run from them, the more persistently they will follow you. Just keep walking forward. You will not suffer when you take a step forward. The more you tell yourself how painful it is, the more you will suffer.

ᏸ 308 ᏸ

If you always try to accept only things that are agreeable to you, someday you will find yourself forced to do things that you do not like. If you persevere through things that you are not fond of doing, and actively strive to build qualities that you thought you did not have, your character will rapidly expand.

✧ 309 ✧

A person who liberates your heart; a person who brightens you and brings out your love for life so that your heart naturally feels gentler and mellower, and more inclined to follow your correct path—that kind of person is the greatest of all.

If you find someone who teaches about spiritual matters, yet restricts others and makes them unfree, that person does not know truth. As the saying goes, 'The truth shall set you free.'

✧ 310 ✧

Some ask whether people of faith are more wonderful than people who do not practice any faith. My answer is that such is not necessarily the case. Some people who have no particular faith are carrying out actions far superior to those of people who do have faith. However, let's suppose that two people are performing actions that are equally splendid, and that one of them practices a faith, while the other does not. When they leave this material plane and go to the spiritual one, there may be a difference. The person who has faith may be able to attain a better situation in the spiritual world, because in addition to reaping the fruits of their own good actions, they can more easily accept the saving grace of their spiritual protectors.

There are splendid people in this world who do not practice any faith. If people who practiced spiritual faith were equally splendid, the result would be even better.

∞ 311 ∞

There is no darkness where the sun shines forth in all its brilliance. Likewise, when your heart is truly filled with a world peace prayer, nothing dark can approach you, and you can never experience misfortune.

∞ 312 ∞

Among the people who come to our prayer group, there are many whom I could train to be first-rate spiritual mediums, if I had a mind to do so. But it is not my intention simply to treat people as tools of the divinities, without regard for their own will and initiative. This is why I have no thought of turning people into spiritual mediums.

✆ 313 ✆

It is good to be honest, but it is not good to flaunt your honesty or pretend that you are honest. The best thing is to simply be straight-out-honest, just as you naturally are.

✆ 314 ✆

Whatever your reasons might be, it is never all right to wage war. Under no circumstances is it justifiable for people to kill one another.

✆ 315 ✆

I always lay my heart bare when I interact with people. I never put on airs or assume any type of posture. I feel that if you can strip your heart bare of all pretense and relate with people spontaneously, without giving them a bad feeling, it shows that you are a person of culture.

✑ 316 ✎

How could God possibly be so foolish as to say, 'All the bad people are agents of the devil, so go ahead and destroy them using whatever weapons you like?' If you hear such words, know that they do not come from God.

✑ 317 ✎

If you have a bright, gentle, loving, optimistic, and care-free disposition, be thankful for it. Pray that you will become even more loving than you are now. Pray that your life will shine even more brightly than it does now. If you do, you will be able to live more and more joyfully and brightly.

✑ 318 ✎

Let us always attune our wavelength to the vibrations of the blue sky.

◄ 319 ►

When you are hesitating over a decision, quiet your thoughts and let your heart be still. Then, pray to your guardian divinity and spirits. They will definitely give you an answer. The only thing is, do not get entrenched in a short-term perspective, caring only about your immediate gains and losses. Even if the answer seems to go against your interests in the short run, put it into practice, just the way it flashed into your consciousness. Even if your present endeavor ends in failure, that answer will definitely bear fruit in the end.

◄ 320 ►

Instead of trying to correct your shortcomings by hammering them out forcibly, pour your energy into expanding your strong points. When you do, your shortcomings will naturally disappear.

∽ 321 ॐ

Train your mind so that you can feel thankful even when you are scolded. Being scolded means that the other person cares about you.

∽ 322 ॐ

A small saint lives concealed in the mountains, while a great saint lives hidden in the town. A great saint is one who can be unattached to dirt while living in dirt, and can live life itself.

∽ 323 ॐ

A wonderful person is someone who can, while they live in this world in their physical body, directly carry out actions that are inspired by their guardian divinity.

∽ 324 ॐ

People sometimes get into discussions about religious theory just for the sake of amusement. It is a mistake to get carried away with side issues, and forget about the essence of spiritual faith. I would like to ask those people to pour their will and their energy into finding out how to rise above karma, how to carry out actions of love, and how to always live brightly and happily with a refreshed feeling.

✧ 325 ✧

When people call you 'teacher,' that is the very time when you ought to closely observe your own thoughts and actions.

✧ 326 ✧

Others will see for themselves whether you are great or not. Just do your best. That is enough.

✧ 327 ✧

It is not good to be in a hurry. Do not expect to achieve your aims in a day. Firmly believe that for a person who lives in the prayer for world peace, the future can never get worse—it is sure to get better. Whatever may appear in front of you, if you steadily pray for world peace with all your heart, and think to yourself that this situation is in the process of fading away, you will always be able to live with composure, regardless of whether your outward situation looks good or bad.

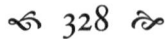

❧ 328 ❧

The practice of 'fading away' is not something that you do yourself, so there is no need to struggle over it or get up tight about it. That kind of approach is mistaken, and it comes from the ego. The ego is not able to clear away the things that are meant to vanish. This is where the existence of your spiritual and divine protectors becomes important. They erase those things for you with their divine love.

❧ 329 ❧

There is nothing that can bring harm to you from the outside. The only things that can bring harm upon you are your own thoughts and feelings. However, those thoughts are in the process of vanishing away.

๑ 330 ๑

If you live your life with the wholehearted desire for peace uppermost in your mind, your guardian divinities and spirits will handle everything perfectly for you.

๑ 331 ๑

Always, always try to polish yourself. There is no limit to a human being's ability to improve.

๑ 332 ๑

When I wholly threw my life into the divine will, thinking 'Even if I don't eat, it's all right,' from that time forward, my path opened up and my spiritual teachings began to take shape.

๑ 333 ๑

One cannot fulfill one's true work unless one's old 'self' dies once and is then reborn as a new person.

∽ 334 ∾

At no time have I felt like becoming a martyr or succumbing to a tragic feeling. Unless you have the kind of mental freedom and composure that allows you to simply hum a tune even in the toughest situation, you cannot carry out your real work as a human being.

∽ 335 ∾

It goes against the divine spirit of the universe to accept or affirm any kind of war as being 'right' or 'just.'

∽ 336 ∾

Even if the so-called 'enemy' were overthrown by a force of arms, a new opponent in a different form would definitely emerge later on. I wonder if people who support a hard-line policy have considered this.

What can be done to bring about true peace in Asia and throughout the world? In the case of Japan, I believe that its role should be to leave aside its own interests for a while, and pursue all matters from a broad, lofty point of view. This is the time for us to think about peace—deeply, thoroughly, and completely.

๑ 337 ๑

To practice spiritual faith is to learn how to nurture an open and artless heart.

๑ 338 ๑

Here are three things that I suggest parents teach and demonstrate to their children:

1. Do not give trouble to others.
2. Take care of your own concerns yourself.
3. When you have some energy to spare, lend a hand to others.

๑ 339 ๑

True teachings do not need a lot of words.

❧ 340 ❧

Parents ought not to scold their children for failing when they have tried to do something good.

❧ 341 ❧

Human beings have a natural desire to be crystal-clear and spotless, like a rapid-running stream.

❧ 342 ❧

You may be able to pull the wool over people's eyes with words or written phrases, but the important thing is the feeling they get when they actually meet you. Become the kind of person who gives people a feeling of warmth and pureheartedness, even without exchanging any words.

❧ 343 ❧

There is no point in comparing the greatness or strength of physical human beings. As physical entities, we are all more or less the same. Everyone's physical consciousness is no more than ordinary.

❧ 344 ❧

If you continue thinking only of others and working only for others, you will naturally be pushed to the forefront, even though you had no thought of attracting people's attention.

❧ 345 ❧

Even if you are tired, that does not justify treating people in a bad-tempered way. Your fatigue or ill-temper has nothing to do with the other person. Always give people a peaceful expression and words filled with love.

❧ 346 ❧

Just being a good person is not enough. You must also put your deep-seated wisdom to work.

⤙ 347 ⤚

Do not attempt things that are beyond your capability. However, once you have committed yourself to a task, follow it through to the end. If, despite your best efforts, you are unable to achieve what you aimed for, apologize frankly, saying that you tried your best, but couldn't do it.

⤙ 348 ⤚

Real patriots or humanitarians never stage revolutions based on political 'isms.' All too often, people engaged in left- or right-wing movements are really just venting their dissatisfaction with their family life, or their living conditions, or the unfulfilled state of their own desires and wishes. Activities of this kind can never turn into movements of true love for one's country or for humanity. They serve only to feed the flames of hatred, conflict, and struggle.

⤙ 349 ⤚

In this world, which of our human ties are founded in true love? The love between marriage partners and lovers is always mingled with self-interest and calculation, and the parties might even vilify one another when their interests do not agree. Friendship does not seem to give us an example of true love either. Where, then, can we see true love? Yes, between mother and child. Only a mother's love never changes. Even if her child turns against her, a mother's love never changes.

⊷ 350 ⊶

A human being should never shrink back passively, saying things like 'I'm too old,' or 'My illness has left me too weak.' In saying such things, you are only making the dent in your heart bigger. You have to move forward. You can only move forward. There is no stepping back. Just keep moving forward, and one day you will reach heaven.

Work more and more for others—the greatest service you can do for others is to work for world peace. If you can add even one person to the number of those who pray for world peace, it is a worthy contribution indeed.

⋖ 351 ⋗

From the viewpoint of your true self, your physical life-time lasts for only a brief instant. Even so, for the duration of that one instant, your true self wishes to make the fullest and best possible use of this physical vessel. That's why I would like all of us to live expansively, without digging up and hashing over our own faults or the faults of others.

⋖ 352 ⋗

What makes good people weak? It is their tendency to exaggerate their weaknesses and mull over their most trifling actions in order to determine whether they were right or wrong. What they ought to be doing instead is to actively expand and build on their good points.

⋖ 353 ⋗

One cannot improve oneself by digging up one's short-comings. It is extremely difficult to eliminate one's short-comings through conscious efforts. If, instead of trying to remove your shortcomings, you plunge deeply into the divine mind that is within you, you will find that your negative qualities have fallen away before you were even aware of it. You might think that this is a slow approach, but actually, it is the quickest way.

✧ 354 ❧

It is not because we cannot bear to give up our physical life that we pray for world peace, nor is it simply because we are afraid of war. We pray because we do not want large numbers of people in many countries to taste the bitterness, anguish, and pain that war causes. We pray because we do not want this earth to lose its existence. We pray because we want the infinite potential of life to manifest itself on this planet.

✧ 355 ❧

Spiritual leaders need to have subtle feelings. A person cannot guide others with a heart made of wire or iron rods.

❧ 356 ❧

The world is constantly in flux. We cannot judge which things are right and good just by observing the trends that show themselves on the surface. That's why we must reflect on things in light of the Way. The Way is, in other words, great harmony. The more confused this world becomes, the more steadfastly we must keep our eyes on the Way.

❧ 357 ❧

There are people who are shining the light of their guardian divinities, even without speaking about religion or God. These are people with a bright, clear, open character.

❧ 358 ❧

If you and your friend cannot openly speak the truth to each other, your friendship is not true. Nurture a friendship so strong that, if your friend is with you, you wouldn't even mind dying.

✥ 359 ✥

Free yourself from disguises and camouflage. When you do, courage, wisdom, power, and all else that you need will come welling up from within you.

✥ 360 ✥

At your workplace, do not fall into sectionalism, thinking 'It's not my department, so it doesn't matter to me.' Instead, try to develop an overall view of the entire workplace. If you fall into the trap of sectionalism, you will not be able to grow at your workplace.

✥ 361 ✥

Do not be in a hurry to make a name for yourself. Those kinds of efforts may end up degrading you. If you need to be famous, the divine will will make you as famous as you need to be.

◈ 362 ◈

Spiritual training is not something that you do through your own efforts. It comes to you naturally. It is not a matter of pushing yourself up to a higher plane. Of course, you do need to have a sincere aim in mind, such as to live for the happiness of others, or to accomplish your divine purpose here on Earth. If you keep thinking this way, your guardian divinities and spirits will guide you to a suitable teacher, and they will bring you to the right place and put you in touch with the right people, so that you will naturally be able to polish and uplift yourself. That is why the first thing I advise people to do is to always give thanks to their guardian divinities and spirits.

◈ 363 ◈

It is really silly to try to show people how powerful you are. If you embark on a path of spiritual training because you wish to attain mysterious powers, hoping that those powers will earn you the respect of others or place you in a higher position than others, then you are on the wrong track and will suffer enormously because of it.

Rather than 'acting,' we are 'acted upon,' or 'acted through.' In matters of spiritual faith, I think we could say that nothing is achieved by the ego.

❧ 364 ❧

Justice is what guides us toward harmony. Justice gives birth to conditions of harmony.

❧ 365 ❧

I never look down on any of the people who come to consult with me, thinking of them only as 'my students' or 'my believers.' I deeply respect each and every one of them.

❧ 366 ❧

Transcending or being free from commonly held assumptions is not the same as lacking common sense. The ideal approach to life is found in anchoring your feet in common sense while letting your mind reach up to heaven.

◈ 367 ◈

Do not be overly concerned with the ups and downs of your karma. That kind of attitude can cause you to chase round and round after your karmic self, so that you end up gradually separating yourself from your true, divine self. What is to occur will occur, what is not to occur will not occur, and what is to fade away will fade away. So, cleanly thrust those concerns out of your mind and plunge yourself wholly into a prayer for world peace. When you do, your mind will feel lighter and brighter, and your fears will disappear.

◈ 368 ◈

Let's open our minds to the message that is radiating from heaven. That message is telling us to throw out old, limiting ideas, like thinking that each of us exists in isolation from others and is different from others.

✧ 369 ✧

As long as people live in this world, they have an almost overpowering tendency to think and act according to their own material interests. When they live this way, it becomes extremely difficult for them to let their lives flow according to the divine will. People need to expand their sense of 'self' beyond the narrow range of their individual concerns to encompass the society, then the nation, then the whole of humanity. Then, from that new vantage-point, they can take a new look at themselves, their society, and the world.

✧ 370 ✧

It takes courage to wholly pursue the way of harmony. In the way of harmony, there is no provision for meeting force with force, or weapons with weapons. To pursue the way of harmony, we need a heart that seeks only truth, and wisdom that discerns the eternity of life.

※ 371 ⁓

I am a realist who has an eternal perspective.

※ 372 ⁓

It is fortunate that you have been gifted with a gentle and acceptant nature. You ought to deepen and expand that wondrous quality, because it is rooted in profound wisdom. This wisdom will come out when you begin to 'act in no-action.'* The great, divine life is constantly supplying our individual lives with wisdom and power that enlivens us and allows us to continually evolve. This is the very same wisdom and power that moves this great universe. What we have to do from the human side is to keep on newly receiving this wisdom and power.

However, it is next to impossible to 'act in no-action' all at once. That is why I guide people in climbing there easily, step by step, through the method of 'Fading away—May peace prevail on Earth.'

* See note after #277.

∽ 373 ҩ

The key that opens the gates of heaven is complete entrustment to the divine. If we rely on our physical power and intellect, we cannot really know anything. We cannot know what awaits us tomorrow, or even one moment from now. Even if we knew what the future held, we would not be able to do anything about it. Our physical existence, in and of itself, can do nothing at all. That is why we leave everything up to the divine and let divine wisdom and power act on our behalf.

∽ 374 ҩ

No matter how poor a family you were born into, no matter how physically weak you might be, and no matter how lacking in talent you might think you are, buds of success will surely appear if you live life in real earnest. I can clearly say this from my own experience. A person who lives in real earnest from moment to moment and day to day will emerge victorious. Each and every human being has been born with some kind of God-given talent.

∾ 375 ∾

It is not good to be over-serious. Sometimes you need to give your mind a rest.

∾ 376 ∾

Someone once asked Goi Sensei 'What is the ideal human personality from the viewpoint of heaven?' Goi Sensei replied—

It's a person who always lends an ear to the voice of heaven.

∾ 377 ∾

I did not come to this world to amuse myself. I came here to manifest the realm of heaven.

∾ 378 ∾

Your life-power will not truly come out if you try to ignite it forcibly. It is not that kind of thing. True life-power is something that naturally wells up from inside.

✍ 379 ✍

What can you do to make your life-power spring up from within? One way would be to read the biographies of saints and great people. If possible, it would be good to make direct contact with holy people and listen to what they say. And if you would add your own prayers on top of that, it would be ideal.

✍ 380 ✍

It is important to create some time each day when you closely observe life.

✍ 381 ✍

It is also important to wait for the right moment. Rather than rushing things or turning over all kinds of thoughts in your mind, it is better to sit still and spend that time praying in your mind.

❧ 382 ❧

If, at this moment, you were told that you had only a short time to live, what would you do? If, while you live, you could devote yourself to assisting others and making them happy, and could face the moment of death with feelings like 'Thank you, everyone!' and 'Excuse me for leaving ahead of you,' how would that be?

There have been a number of things said about 'enlightenment' or 'awakening,' but a person who can live and die in the way I have just described is what I would call 'awakened.'

❧ 383 ❧

Love is patience.

❧ 384 ❧

Disrupting harmony is the same as defiling the divine mind. For example, suppose you are in the right and the other person is in the wrong. If the person makes unreasonable demands on you or treats you harshly, you might easily think, 'What a jerk! I'd like to get even with him!' Generally speaking, this feeling is considered natural. However, to react in this way unsettles your own heart, which means that you are hurting yourself. To hurt yourself is the same as defiling the divine mind. You might say the other person is at fault, but your reaction did not come from the other person. It concerns you alone.

No matter how bad the other person might be, and no matter how spitefully he or she may treat you, if you send out waves of anger or resentment, it disturbs your own divine mind, which is not in keeping with the universal will. I explain to people that these kinds of emotions are karmic effects that come out in the process of fading away. When this kind of emotion is pushed out from inside you, brought to the surface triggered by some incident, think of it as 'fading away' and fling it into a prayer. Just pray intently and allow it to disappear.

❧ 385 ❧

Some people may be thinking: 'I have been doing my utmost to be of service to others, yet they treat me appallingly.' What I suggest to them is this: think that your guardian spirits are allowing this to happen in order to uncover and increasingly draw out your divinity. Believe that you are making great leaps toward joyfulness.

❧ 386 ❧

Everything that rises to the surface came about through causes and effects from our past lifetimes. Although you are in no way being unkind to someone now, somewhere in your thoughts from the past there was an element of unkindness toward them. Otherwise, there would be no grounds for their ill-treatment of you now. That is the law of cause and effect. If you keep on perpetuating these cycles, the waves of discord will never subside.

However unpleasant your situation, never unsettle your own mind. Never hurt another person. Until this principle is understood, true peace will not come about on Earth, and human beings will not achieve their spiritual peace and stability.

❧ 387 ❧

People with a brisk and optimistic disposition should thank heaven for it.

✥ 388 ✥

The following is a conversation someone had with Goi Sensei—

—Sensei, I feel that the leaders of the future need to put their own lives in order before they attempt anything else. What would you say is the most important quality for a leader?

—It's bigheartedness.

—Can we acquire bigheartedness through conscious effort?

—Not so much through conscious effort as through opening up your heart. As you let your heart expand, you naturally become bighearted.

—What can we do if we want to become more expansive and bighearted?

—Just entrust everything completely to the divine will. Just believe that since God is love, there is never a mistake in what the divine will does.

✄ 389 ✄

When I was young I was very earnest in my search for truth. Whether I was walking along the street, or whatever I was doing, I would say 'Thank you, God.' From morning to night, whether waking or sleeping, I would continually say 'Thank you, God,' in much the same way as all of you say 'May peace prevail on Earth.'

My mind was densely packed with the words 'Thank you, God.' Even if someone happened to kick me, the only words that escaped my lips were 'Thank you, God.' No other thought came to mind. Even when I experience physical pain, I only think 'Thank you, God.' It is not that I make a special effort to do this—it is just that nothing else comes to mind.

✄ 390 ✄

Here is what Goi Sensei experienced when he was still in his spiritual training.* He had a large boil on his foot, and it was giving him terrible pain. It was the rush hour, and the train was so crammed with passengers that some nearly fell out. Suddenly, someone kicked Goi Sensei in the foot, right on the boil, yet the

only words that slipped from his mouth were 'Thank you.'
Ordinarily, in that situation I feel sure that most people would
think 'Ouch!' or 'You clumsy fool!' or something like that. How
wonderful it must be to always feel thankful, whatever might
happen, right on the spot. Whenever I recall this story, I fervent-
ly wish that all of us could behave like that.

* See note after #305.

࿇ 391 ࿇

When Goi Sensei was in his spiritual training,* an ethereal voice
whispered in his ear, saying, 'You will accomplish feats that even
Buddha or Jesus could not do. Such is the power that you hold! You
are the one and only, greatest savior this earth has known!' Goi
Sensei was not a bit impressed by this voice. Had he been taken in
by it, the immaculate efforts he had made until then would have
crumbled and vanished into nothingness. In other words, for him
to continue along his appointed path, his soul was not allowed to
harbor even one speck of dirt or vanity. Goi Sensei rejected all
those whisperings, saying—

No, I am not like that. It doesn't matter to me if I am a
small savior or a big savior. My only wish is to act in accor-

dance with the divine will.

Goi Sensei often told us—

Do not be careless enough to fall for those kinds of unearthly whisperings. Even if it is a test given to you by your guardian divinity, if you are taken in by it, it means you have flunked the test. Be very careful not to fall prey to pride and arrogance.

   * See note after #305.

✧ 392 ✧

Here is one thing that happened while I was undergoing spiritual training.* My guardian divinity ordered me to cross a big thoroughfare with my eyes shut. Though the cars were rushing back and forth along the 26-meter wide road, I tried to cross it with my eyes shut, just as I had been told. Yet when I tried to take a step, my legs would not move from the sidewalk. I thought I had flunked my test. Try as I might, I could not cross the road. My guardian divinity scolded me then, saying, 'What a silly goose you are! Who on Earth would cross a road with his eyes closed?'

THE WISDOM OF MASAHISA GOI

When you are in doubt, use your head and judge for
yourself whether this would be a reasonable thing to do or
not. If you cannot make up your mind, no matter how
hard you may think about it, then you should move in ac-
cordance with the divine will. This is how I was trained by
my guardian divinity. And these experiences of mine gave
birth to my teaching: 'Rise above common sense without
derailing from common sense.'

* See note after #305.

ঔ 393 ৵

Here is another experience that I had during my spiritual
training.* In those days, my guardian divinity was leading
me around in circles. There was a period when I was pre-
sented with a string of downright lies, over and over again.
Even so, I never once felt annoyed by this. One day, my
guardian divinity gave me a detailed prediction about
what would happen to a certain person, and I even repeat-
ed it to the person in question. When the prediction
turned out to be totally false, rather than feeling conster-
nation, I was jubilant about it. I realized at that moment
that high-ranking divinities would never offer us that sort

of detailed prediction about the trivial events in a person's life.

Never did I feel even the slightest doubt in the wisdom of my guardian divinity's guidance, because I had already entrusted myself wholly to that guidance. In other words, I was able to smoothly accept the way of truth. Thanks to the precious training that I received, I honed my ability to discern right from wrong, and truth from falsehood.

* See note after #305.

◆ 394 ◆

In another phase of my spiritual training,* I was caused to transcribe, through automatic writing, various divine revelations in the name of a famous divinity. However, I did not gulp them down whole, believing in everything that had been written. I simply considered this assignment as a kind of warm-up exercise to facilitate communication with the divine world, and paid no attention to the contents.

* See note after #305.

☞ 395 ☜

A magazine called Face *ran a feature article entitled 'The True Face of Masahisa Goi and the Byakko Shinko Kai.' In that article, they cited an interview with Goi Sensei done by Dr. Kazuo Kasahara, who has a Ph.D. in Literature and works as an assistant professor at Tokyo University. In this interview, Dr. Kasahara asked Goi Sensei, 'How did it happen that you reached your spiritual awakening?' Below is Goi Sensei's answer—*

In my case, my true self was awakened as I was gazing at the sun. I was walking beside the Nakagawa (Naka River), and somehow, I felt like looking at the sun. So, I sat down right then and there to look at the sun. Then, all of a sudden, everything around me was transformed into a pure, white light. At that time, I clearly heard a divine voice saying 'I have received your life.' That was how it began.

I (H. Takahashi) was present at the interview, and heard what was said directly. I had previously heard Goi Sensei tell of his experience by the Nakagawa, but I did not recall ever having heard the words 'my true self was awakened as I was gazing at the sun.' Later, when I mentioned this to Goi Sensei, he replied—

Oh, didn't you? Well, yes, that was how it was. As I was gazing intently at the sun, the divinity of the sun appeared to me from within the sun. In a twinkling, its image multiplied into a great many, then got bigger and bigger until everything merged into a sheer, white light. At that moment, an irresistibly powerful vibration, or voice, was felt. The voice thundered: 'I have received your life. Are you prepared?' I instantly replied, 'Yes, I am.' It was then that my spiritual training* began.'

    * See note after #305.

⤚ 396 ⤙

When people walk along the street, they think that their physical bodies are walking, but that is not really true. *Goi Sensei suddenly said this to me one day out of the blue, in a very amused manner, as we were walking along the street.*

Who do you think is walking now? *he asked, but I could not answer.*

During my spiritual training,* one day, as I was walking along the street, my spiritual being suddenly expanded, and numerous divinities merged into it and walked along with me. On another day, my spiritual being got taller and taller, lifting my consciousness to an extremely high place, while my physical body continued walk on its own. I have had quite a variety of experiences like this, and so I am well aware that I am not walking on physical power.

In thinking of this, I recall another comment that Goi Sensei had made previously—

When I get tired, I let my legs walk on their own. If your head aches or your vision is poor, it has nothing to do with your walking.

* See note after #305.

๛ 397 ๖

My mother—the sage.

From my mother, I received the gift of sincerity. I can remember her telling me: 'Never give trouble to others,' and 'Never borrow money.' And from her, I also inherited a steadfast spirit. She once had a terrible boil on her foot. Even so, she maintained an unperturbed expression and continued to work, moving the aching foot around forcefully on purpose. She had a truly firm character. She did not think of illness as being illness, and she was convinced that she would never die of illness. She used to say in her clear-cut way, 'Illness will be cured when it is time for it to be cured—and if it is not cured, it will be your time to die.'

She took a long-term view of everything.

~§ 398 §~

Even when I was in my thirties, when I visited my mother, she would always say, 'Now, stretch out your feet and I'll wash them.' She did this to all of her sons. Bringing a bucket and a washcloth, she would make us sit on the edge of the veranda and have our feet washed.

'You don't need to do that, Mom, I can do it myself,' we would tell her. But she would insist, saying 'Don't be silly. Your feet are dirty. Come now, stretch them out.' She still seemed to think of us as little children.

One day, I heard that she had spoken to the neighbors about it with great pleasure, saying: 'My sons still come home and have their feet washed!' After I heard this, I decided not to put up a struggle anymore. From then on, I would just obediently let her wash my feet, then say, 'Thank you, Mom.'

✤ 399 ✤

One morning, a few days after the passing of Goi Sensei's mother, a gentleman named K. Ichikawa, whose own mother had passed away a year before, came to visit Goi Sensei and express his condolences. With tears streaming from his eyes, Mr. Ichikawa could find no words to say except, 'I know... I know...' As Goi Sensei's tears came spilling out, he too was unable to say anything more than, 'Yes...Yes...'

Goi Sensei later told me—

Until then, I had managed to hold back my tears, but when I saw Mr. Ichikawa's tears, I could hold mine back no longer.

✤ 400 ✤

Here is a story that Goi Sensei told one morning to the people who had gathered to hear him speak—

My mother loved to eat crushed ice in the summer. I did not care much for crushed ice myself, but she would ask again and again for me to go with her and have some. 'Just one cup,' she would say, 'Oh, please, come with me.' So, I would go to the shop with her, reluctantly. But one cup was never enough for her, and she would ask, 'Do you think I could order a second cup?' Of course I would answer, 'Sure, Mom, you can have as many as you like.' Sometimes, as they get up in years, mothers like to be pampered by their children. When I saw how cute she looked enjoying her second cup of crushed ice, it brought tears to my eyes.

Having said this, Goi Sensei fell silent for a while. I glanced up at him and saw the tears trickling down his cheek. And during the next few moments, little sobs could be heard here and there throughout the audience.

❧ 401 ❧

Your greatest benefactor in this world is your mother. It is no easy matter to give birth to a child and help it grow up. That is why, even if some people might think her silly or unsophisticated, I respect a woman who has borne and raised a child.

www.ingramcontent.com/pod-product-compliance
Lightning Source LLC
Chambersburg PA
CBHW060320050426
42449CB00011B/2579